LISTEN
PRAY
CARE

LISTEN PRAY CARE

Hack the Code of Love
Bust Up Boring Pews
And Sport the Disciple Tattoo

ALAN KLATT

ISBN: 978-1-7338846-0-0

Cover design: David Hahn

Printed in the United States of America.
2019—First Edition

10 9 8 7 6 5 4 3 2 1

Sola Amor Publishing
W355N5674 Lisbon Rd.
Oconomowoc, WI 53066

www.ListenPrayCare.org

DEDICATION

To Mom and Dad, for listening in love.

CONTENTS

ACKNOWLEDGMENTS

I would like to thank

God for his love, mercy, and faithfulness, and especially
for the gift of his Son, Jesus Christ who has made
God's love real to me.

Robert Nugent for your amazing ability to create
relatable examples out of thin air and persistent and
passionate pursuit of a relationship with God.

Todd Radke for using your remarkable encouragement
and editing gifts to bring the words of this book to life.

David Hahn for your unending enthusiasm for the
task of speaking to new generations and for sharing your
artistic design talents.

Mike Duehr for your faithful support and patience in
conversations over coffee about the Bible and the
possibilities for the church of the future.

My children, for helping me see the long view, and
encouraging me to keep going despite
the length of the journey.

Family and friends that assisted with the editing of this
book, especially Alisa Klatt, Melody Klatt, Christiana
Klatt, Benjamin Klatt, Tiffany Klatt, Rev. Eberhard Klatt,
Betty Klatt, Dr. Ruth Seabaugh, Amy Tassoul,
Laura Radke, and Kristal Nugent.

INTRODUCTION

In the spring of 2011, I was sitting at my desk in my office. Father's Day weekend was over—always a big event in my family with eight children. I had just finished putting the final touches on a six week sermon series on Ephesians. I also had made some phone calls and was preparing for the next day's Bible study. Once I was finished, I would make a quick trip to the grocery store before dinner.

That's when it hit me.

An *idea.*

I was suddenly unable to concentrate on the Bible study. I grabbed a notebook and began jotting down my thoughts.

God was working on me. Simple questions about God's love were becoming something significantly bigger: a vision for a new approach to loving one another as Jesus directed.

I could see everyone participating: young and old, people from every language and culture, in big groups and small, in schools and churches, at sporting events and in homes.

It was difficult to figure out the simplest way to move toward the goal. How do we *explain* the practice of loving our neighbor? How do we make it practical for any setting—wherever two or three are gathered? In our homes, coffee shops, churches, youth groups, classrooms, or sports teams?

Love is such an abstract concept. How do we talk about it in a concrete way? We experience love as a feeling, but what are the most basic human *actions* that get us started on the path to loving relationships?

I challenged myself. If I could not explain loving one another in the simplest terms, how could I teach it to children? To parents? In youth group? To the coach of my daughter's Christian volleyball team?

I was convinced we needed a short and universal starting point for everyone committed to loving others. It would need to be easy to explain, effective, and able to be practiced by *anyone*, especially in relationships with and among children.

Relationships in our Christian gatherings would become healthier. Our relationally-wired generations would be more willing to engage. Our changing, transitioning, and even declining churches would be positively impacted. And relief would come to overburdened leaders in their care for God's people.

So that summer the project began. I began to put the ideas, vision, and plans God was giving me into creative resources like this book.

Now, the critical role of love in the Christian life and message is not new. Its importance and impact is highlighted by recent authors—Francis Chan *Crazy Love*, Henry Blackaby *Experiencing God's Love in the Church: The Missing Ingredient in Today's Church and How to Bring It Back*, Gerald Sittser *Love One Another: Becoming the Church Jesus Longs For*, Alexander Strauch *Love or Die: Christ's Wake-Up Call to the Church*, and Rick Warren *40 Days of Love: We Were Made for Relationships*.

I am not trying to reinvent the wheel. The challenge of loving others is continuous and obvious, but I believe we need a new way to approach it. Simple. Concrete. Easy to understand and remember.

It is my hope that you, the reader, will find this book a helpful tool in your search for the best ways to share God's love in your personal life and wherever he calls you to lead.

Section 1

Setting the Stage

1
THE MUSIC
LIKE A SYMPHONY GONE BAD

Music is a part of every culture on earth. Whether primal or sophisticated, it moves us and speaks the language of the soul.

I personally love the classic symphony orchestra. Orchestras work hard to sound beautiful, play harmoniously, and delightfully draw the audience into their music. It requires each player to be on the same page, to play in concert with the whole orchestra, and to follow the lead of the conductor.

Bad things happen when an orchestra doesn't work right.

Even the novice listener can tell when something goes wrong. If the brass players hit the wrong notes or if the string players play at the wrong tempo, you can tell. It isn't pretty. Instead of harmony, you have dissonance. Instead of beauty and wonder, you have discord and chaos. Smiles turn to frowns in the audience. People want the noise to stop. People won't come back. They will seek the sound they love elsewhere.

The same thing happens in church. Church is designed to be beautiful, harmonious, and inspiring. However, that is not always the case. When things go wrong, people do not like it. They leave to find harmony elsewhere.

We struggle to convince people of the church's relevance in daily life. Some claim we are now in a post-Christian culture. I personally do not believe that God and church are more or less obsolete. I do admit that our *symphony* in church may, at times, produce noticeably discordant noise. People sometimes see our attempts at relational harmony, cringe, and walk away.

In my observations, churches have always struggled with unhealthy behaviors and distractions. Historically, church leaders and followers contribute to the chaos and discord by getting off-message and engaging in conflict. Conflict leads to man-made crusades, often brother-against-brother, with banners from both sides sporting God's name hastily scrawled at the bottom. It is painful. Dissonant. Our music sounds like noise.

I awakened to our struggling symphony as the Body of Christ during my visits with brothers and sisters in the faith, who believe current trends in the Church do not bode well for the future of the Church. I believe a big contributor to church decline is the public disconnect between the verbal message in our gatherings and the love we show for one another.

Here is an example. We can attend weekend services or other Christian activities for years, even decades, without directly sharing God's love in Christ with the people sitting around us. Given Christ's command to love one another, something is wrong. The symphony does not sound right. We focus on fervently building our relationship with God, but weakly build relationships with each other.

Listen to the voices of our young people today. Many fail to see how church on Sundays makes a difference in personal or global relational conflicts—injustice, wars, and violence. They see church as relationally irrelevant and even contributing to problems. Something is wrong if their only hope for the future is the complete absence of conflict. The Gospel teaches about a peace that is found in the midst of human conflict.

Our children will not expect church to significantly change the world if they are unable to see the difference the church makes in their lives and relationships first. It starts in our Christian gatherings, no matter the size or setting.

It is a sad day when we no longer believe in the church's greatest treasure—God's love in Christ saving us, and shaping and building our relationships with each other.

Mahatma Gandhi, during his fight for freedom using passive resistance, sprinkled his core message with the need for love as the foundation for all human relationships. He said, "Peace between countries must rest on the solid foundation of love between individuals."

Civil rights advocate Dr. Martin Luther King Jr. in his sermon at Dexter Avenue Baptist Church in Montgomery, Alabama on November 17, 1957 addressed his congregation with these words: "Yes, it is love that will save our world and our civilization, love even for enemies." Dr. King saw the potential of God's love and made it the core of his message.

Our emerging Christian generations are expecting to engage in more than a personal relationship with God. They want to experience God in the middle of real, live, authentic, messy, and complicated human relationships. They want the whole experience. They want their relationship with God to make a tangible, ongoing difference in their personal relationships with people around them. It seems natural. It seems right.

Our discussions of relationships in the symphony of mankind start with the fact that we are created by God for loving relationships with others.

The account of the creation of man in the Bible's narrative highlights the first relationship between humans:

> The LORD God said, 'It is not good for the man to
> be alone. I will make a helper suitable for him'.
> (Genesis 2:18)

You might remember that in Genesis all creation was declared *good*, with one exception. Being alone. Man was not created to be alone. God said it was not good. God's solution was to create a woman, Eve, to be in a close, loving relationship with Adam as his wife (Genesis 2:21-22).

Take note. The symphony of the family of God was not right and good until Adam had a companion. He was placed in a personal relationship designed by God.

Our relationships with each other are not simply random competition with those who would threaten our survival. We are meant for more. We are meant to be together. We are meant to be in harmonious relationships with others.

However, Adam and Eve fell into sin. The descendants of Adam and Eve—our world's entire population—became relationally distant, harsh, and discordant.

My own life experience is proof. I was mugged as a teen riding on a bike trail in Milwaukee. As a young child, I also had the experience of being bullied on a regular basis. Thankfully, the bullying ceased when my big, tough, older sister intervened.

How about you? Is your story a beautiful symphony of human relationships, or are there close encounters with the reality of human sinfulness?

Since people can be cold, ruthless, and unforgiving, we might entertain the idea that being alone is *better* than being with people. This is contrary to the created order. Admittedly, there are times I have felt this way.

We can be pushed toward the conclusion that no one can be trusted and that life is all about surviving our neighbors versus serving them.

We might begin thinking we are here to compete and win. Worse, some conclude that we should just end ourselves and die.

At minimum, we find ourselves turning away, or at least hesitating when called upon to relate to people around us. We may restrict ourselves to cool, impersonal and business-like relationships.

We were not *created* to live this way. We were set on the course of love. We were created to love with our whole heart, mind, and strength.

Love is so powerful that if everyone lived in love, our world would be at peace. There would be a beautiful symphony of humanity making music in perfect harmony.

ALONE IN CHURCH

One day, I was feeling terrible. A close family member was dying. A good friend with a wife and young kids just lost his job. Hurtful rumors about me were circulating.

6

I was grieving. I was in pain. I was away from my family on a business trip. I was uncomfortable.

I was alone.

I was aching for human love and care as I drove to an unfamiliar church on that miserable day. I needed help and love from people who, I assumed, understood how to help a fellow human being in a hurting and broken world. The building was beautiful. The parking lot was full. I opened the door and entered alone...

And I left alone.

Reflecting on my experience later, a phrase kept going through my mind, "They didn't love me." It wasn't because I was alone in the physical sense--there were lots of people--but I felt the people *left* me alone. They did nothing to care about me or even get to know me.

Maybe it was partly my fault, or their fault. Perhaps, it was their leader's fault. Maybe there was something I was supposed to do. Maybe I was supposed to fill out a card or something. Maybe I was supposed to say something. Maybe leaving me to myself was to avoid offending me and make me more likely to stay—like mattress shopping with no sales pressure.

But, in my time of need, I felt I was alone in the most important way. The people around me weren't there for me. I am not saying they *wouldn't* spiritually love or care about me. They just didn't.

This brings me to the subject of the necessity and relevance of church.

A fellow Christian recently commented, "I've left my church too. Mostly because I felt more lonely there than not there."

Consider this proposition. *A world without God should find God in church.* Here is its corollary. *A world without love should find love in church.* Does my local church want my soul saved? Yes. Sure. Do they want to love and care for me in my complicated, ongoing brokenness? Yes. I think so. Do they know how? Not really. Honestly, they probably don't even think about it.

One of my daughters had similar feelings about her select volleyball team. She said that they did tons of stuff together, but she was basically alone. Her teammates were all about volleyball, which was good for the game, but they were not really relational. She put it this way, "I would not call my teammates my friends, at all." The coach confirmed the idea when she argued that there was no time for meaningful friendships. The coach focused on creating a winning volleyball team. And they won.

The argument could be made that her volleyball team did what volleyball teams do—play volleyball. But are sports only about winning on the court or field? What are we teaching our young people if that is the case?

What do you believe is the intent and purpose of our Christian gatherings? I believe we are whole-heartedly committed to communicating the message of God's love in Christ. We also are committed to expressing love for God in our worship music.

However, we have little time to intentionally and deliberately love one another. Our love for one another is generally limited to greetings, corporate prayers and periodic exhortations to love one another. As a result, we miss out on the full experience of loving one another as Christ loved us.

THE MAN IN THE PEW

One Sunday morning in the large church I was serving as pastor, my attention turned to a middle-aged man in attendance. Since I was a newly installed pastor, I hadn't met him yet. Each Sunday, he seemed to find his way out of the church through a different door, so I did not have the chance to greet him. I decided to speak to a lady who sat in the same row.

"Good morning," I said.

"Good morning, Pastor," she replied.

"I want to ask you about the gentleman who sits by himself in your pew. I noticed he didn't appear very happy this morning."

"Oh, yes. I see him once in a while," she said, fidgeting a bit.

"I haven't met him yet," I said. "Do you know his name?"

"Oh dear," she responded, "come to think of it, I haven't had the chance to speak with him yet. He seems very nice."

When I spoke with other people who sat near the man in the pew, it turned out they had good things to say. He seemed nice, polite, and he sang nicely. Most of them said they knew him for years, but they really didn't *know* him. Nobody could tell me his name.

After several visits with the man, I learned he was struggling with a health issue that caused him constant pain. He was also struggling with loneliness, being at home by himself. Yet, as far as I could determine, he only shared pleasantries with the people in our church. No one had a conversation with him about what was going on in his life.

In my first visit with him, I mentioned his anonymity and he responded, "No offense, but I don't go to church for the people, I go for God. I don't expect people to bother with me. And they don't. And I certainly don't bother other people with anything personal about me."

The answer felt wrong. It was not what I expected. I felt like we were a self-serve carwash where cars are cleaned without the hassle of human interaction. Human interaction is not a hassle, it is part of the overall goal of our gatherings according to Christ. Or at least should be.

It is time to revisit our goals and methods of engaging God's people in loving one another in our gatherings and admit we may need to try something new.

In a symphony gone bad, it helps to determine if a major fix of the whole orchestra is needed or a minor adjustment of one or two instruments.

If love for one another in church is like making music, right now it sounds like the entire orchestra hasn't been practicing their parts. They only play a little here and there, if at all.

To the listener, the music sounds awful. Audiences shrink. To the conductor, it signals that something needs fixing.

2
THE MAKER
CREATED TO LOVE

God created us to love. However, we cannot truly love without God. In the beginning, God's Spirit flowed in and through us endlessly. We overflowed with love that comes from the heart of God. Love was the preeminent fruit of the Spirit of God in all his children. Originally, you could recognize God the Father in every loving word and action of his children. We truly were images of his love.

People say I look like my sainted father. If you look at a picture of us, you would definitely see the similarities. Some of my father is in me. My appearance, mannerisms and even voice are like his.

God is our heavenly Father. We are expected to talk, look, and act like him because this is the way he made us. His Spirit flows in and through us. We reflect the heart of God in our words and actions.

This is the way it is supposed to be.

THE HEART OF GOD

In Psalm 136, we get a glimpse of the heart of our Father expressed by the psalm writer in the refrain *His love endures forever*:

> [God] by his understanding made the heavens,
> His love endures forever.
>
> who spread out the earth upon the waters,
> His love endures forever.
>
> who made the great lights—
> His love endures forever.
>
> the sun to govern the day,
> His love endures forever.
>
> the moon and stars to govern the night;
> His love endures forever. (Psalm 136:5-9)

God's love is widespread—it fills the earth:

> The LORD loves righteousness and justice;
> the earth is full of his unfailing love.
> (Psalm 33:5)
>
> The earth is filled with your love, LORD.
> (Psalm 119:64a)

God has a heart of love. God's love is enduring and far reaching:

> Your love, LORD, reaches to the heavens,
> your faithfulness to the skies. (Psalm 36:5)

LOVE GIVES

What is God's love like? In the Old Testament language of the Bible, the root of the Hebrew word for love, *av*, means *to give.* This provides us with an insight into love—love gives. God manifests the giving nature of love when he gives his love to us.

Without God's love, the results of the fall of man recorded in Genesis chapter 3 would be permanent and tragic. Wrath and punishment for man's problem with sin is all we could expect from God (Romans 6:23a). We all die. Yet, God gives us a message of hope. His heart of love changes the picture. There is a light in the darkness found in his love for us. Love is in his creative work and, even more importantly, in his redemptive work.

In the Old Testament Moses reminded the children of Israel of God's nature and motive to save them:

> [God] *loved* your ancestors and chose their
> descendants after them, he brought you out of
> Egypt by his Presence and his great strength.
> (Deuteronomy 4:37, emphasis mine)

> It was because the LORD *loved* you.... Know
> therefore that the LORD your God is God; he is the
> faithful God, keeping his covenant of *love* to a
> thousand generations of those who *love* him and
> keep his commandments. The LORD your God will
> keep his covenant of *love* with you, as he swore to
> your ancestors. He will *love* you and bless you.
> (Deuteronomy 7:8b-9,12b-13a, emphasis mine)

Is God loving and compassionate? God revealed his heart of love to Moses:

> The LORD, the LORD, the compassionate and
> gracious God, slow to anger, abounding in
> love and faithfulness, maintaining love to
> thousands, and forgiving wickedness, rebellion
> and sin. (Exodus 34:6b-7a)

God's love was flowing in and through his actions from the beginning. This includes the creation of the world, the saving of the Israelites from slavery in Egypt, and the saving of mankind from the second death through Christ. God poured out his love in and through Christ in a new and beautiful testament for all to see:

> For God so *loved* the world that he *gave* his one
> and only Son. (John 3:16a, emphasis mine)

> But God demonstrates his own love for us in this:
> While we were still sinners, Christ died for us.
> (Romans 5:8)

> Because of his great love for us, God, who is rich in mercy, made us alive with Christ even when we were dead in transgressions—it is by grace you have been saved. (Ephesians 2:4)

> This is how God showed his love among us: he sent his one and only Son into the world that we might live through him. This is love: not that we loved God, but that he loved us and sent his Son as an atoning sacrifice for our sins.
> (1 John 4:9-10)

God's heart of love is behind *all* the saving acts of God toward man. This is the Good News. Without God's love, there are no acts of grace, mercy, sacrifice or forgiveness. Without God's love, we never stand a chance to have a relationship with God. Without God's love, we are left with our own works which are inadequate before God.

Thankfully, our loving God saves us. The heart of God is love.

John summarized it perfectly:

> "God is love." (1 John 4:8b)

MY FATHER LOVES ME

Who are we? John was inspired to say:

> See what great love the Father has lavished on us, that we should be called children of God! And that is what we are! (1 John 3:1a)

17

Throughout history, human beings have pondered the deepest questions about life. *Know Thyself* is a popular aphorism in Greek literature. Each new generation pursues the path to discover the truth about who we are.

God our Father loves each one of his children.

A father's love for his children is a very powerful thing. I should know. When my eight children were little, I tangibly experienced the true meaning of chaos from day to day. Out of the chaos came questions. Each child asked important questions to try to understand their father. They were seeking to know themselves by learning how I loved them.

Here is an example of how this would take place in my home:

> Out of nowhere an innocent question would be repeated in our home from time to time, "Dad, do you love me more than anyone in the world?"
>
> An indirect answer wouldn't suffice—especially given the many sneaky eavesdroppers hiding from view. I would answer, "Yes, I love you more than anyone in the whole, wide world."
>
> "Thanks Dad!" was the ecstatic reply. I would then receive an enthusiastic hug.
>
> Then a different voice would speak up from a hiding place and say, "What about me?"

> I would turn my attention toward the little voice and say, "Well, I love *you* more than anyone in the whole, wide world." Another hug would come my way.
>
> Then another voice would speak up and say, "What about me?" and I would answer the same way, and so on.

It was a solid truth for my children. I was telling them that I didn't just love them collectively. I loved each one of them individually with all my love. They were my children, and nothing could change how much I loved them. I loved them with my whole heart.

They were learning that love from their dad was not divided or limited in supply. Their father's love was complete and infinite—for each child.

As I look back, I was doing what I was supposed to be doing. I was reflecting my heavenly Father by the way I showed love for my children.

God pours out his love in us and, when we pour out love, we begin to look like God our Father. We are meant to be reflections of our loving Father through our loving actions, just like Jesus. He is our best example. It gives new meaning to *the apple doesn't fall far from the tree.*

We were created *for* love.

In the beginning, Adam and Eve were created in the image of God (Genesis 1:26-27). My friends and

colleagues join in lively debates over *exactly* what this means. Some say it means authority and rule. Others say, perfection.

Me? I believe the image of the heart of God is revealed when I love God and others in my words and actions. I love like my heavenly Father. I show love like Jesus did.

I made some sketches depicting our relationship with God. God pours love into us as a free gift through Christ and the Holy Spirit. As a result, we are filled to overflowing with his love and we, in turn, pour out love toward God and others.

Paul described the source of our love and how we receive it:

> Hope does not put us to shame, because God's
> love has been poured out into our hearts through
> the Holy Spirit. (Romans 5:5a)

THE GREATEST IS LOVE

Love is a matter of the heart, and love is at the heart of what matters to God. When God's love pours into us through his Spirit, love is supposed to pour out in all our actions toward God and neighbor. According to God, it is the supreme fruit we bear.

We see this in the commands, laws, decrees and stipulations of God. God's commands are his method of telling us the way things are supposed to be. Through Moses, God revealed his most important expectations in two great commandments:

> Hear, O Israel: The LORD our God, the LORD is one.
> Love the LORD your God with all your heart and
> with all your soul and with all your strength.
> (Deuteronomy 6:4-5)

> Love your neighbor as yourself.
> (Leviticus 19:18b)

Through the Holy Spirit, Paul wrote in a similar vein:

> And now these three remain: faith, hope and
> love. But the greatest of these is love.
> (1 Corinthians 13:13)

> Do everything in love. (1 Corinthians 16:14)

Love is a powerful thing. It shapes our understanding of who God is and who he made us to be. It truly is the foundation to understanding ourselves—our origin, our makeup, and our purpose.

Since God has poured out his love in us through his Spirit, we overflow and pour out love for him and for others. We were created *to be loved* by God and each other, and *to love* God and one another. That is who we are. Love is at the core of our faith relationship with God.

According to Paul, everything boils down to one thing:

> The only thing that counts is faith expressing itself through love. (Galatians 5:6b)

John, one of the most prolific of the Bible writers on the subject of love, clearly states God's purpose for us:

> Love comes from God. (1 John 4:7b)

> We love because he first loved us. (1 John 4:19)

> Since God so loved us, we also ought to love... (1 John 4:11)

> Everyone who loves has been born of God and knows God. (1 John 4:7c)

OUR SIGNIFICANCE

We were created to love, and be loved, as members of God's family forever. As we discover this truth, God our Father leads us to answers for the deepest questions about ourselves. He identifies us. He gives us our purpose. He gives us our family—genetically and spiritually. He gives us our future.

On the journey toward maturity, we learn to answer questions about our identity, purpose, family and future by reflecting what God says about us.

Here is a summary of the basic questions:

- **Identity** – The question: Who am I? The answer: A child created, loved and saved by God.

- **Purpose** – The question: Why am I here? The answer: I am here to love God and others.

- **Family** – The question: To whom do I belong? The answer: I belong to the family of God.

- **Future** – The question: Where is my life ultimately going? The answer: I will live forever with the family of God in heaven.

Look at this in contrast to what the secular world teaches about our significance:

- **Identity** – I am the result of an entirely random spark of life.

- **Purpose** – My purpose is to survive and thrive at any cost.

- **Family** – My family is made up of those who help me fulfill my purpose.

- **Future** – My future is to be remembered by others. Or not.

It does not surprise me that we have a world filled with people who view their lives as dismal, disharmonic, disconnected and dark. This is our world without love. Without love, the music we make as humans is not neutral. It is grating, ugly, and painful.

Every generation actively searches for answers to life's biggest questions. Some of us are not satisfied by trite, secular answers, or the spiritually empty views of internet prophets. We believe there is something more. We might look to the stars. We might try to embrace the force or energy that moves through us in this life, determining our outcome, fate or destiny. We might put our faith in the fates, gods, the devil, Mother Nature, karma, luck, or aliens.

The many manmade religions of our world show a global human pursuit of supernatural answers to who we are and why we are here.

In every case, though, we eventually end up feeling lost and alone. When we can't find ourselves. Others ultimately don't matter. We are alone, surrounded by lost people.

Yet, every one of us is designed to live as family, under God. He made us. He is the one who finds us and reveals himself to us through his Son, by his Spirit.

Without God, the people of our world are truly without love. Without love, we have no peace or harmony. All we have is a noisy, disturbing cacophony.

CARDBOARD ALTRUISM

Altruism is benefitting others without expectation of reward, even at cost to self. Altruism supposedly proves the existence of true love to the world filled with excellent observers and poor interpreters.

Altruism apart from God, however, is only a cardboard cutout of the real thing. Like earthly success, it sure can look attractive. However, as self-perceived beauty plus a cold heart equal vanity, altruism without God's love is only a pretty shell.

The attractiveness of altruism is in its selfless, sacrificial giving which is only a shadow of God's true love. Altruism extends all the way from dropping a few cents toward the benefit of the homeless, to martyrdom. Poor interpreters make the argument that there is essentially no need for God's love, since we have a heroic, honorable version of pure love found in altruism.

Here is the truth. Altruism does not require love at all. It can come out of selfless, detached, and disinterested motives. A person may rescue someone drowning in a swimming pool at great risk to themselves. In the final analysis, they simply may be a heroic, godless altruist who felt *it was the right thing to do,* absent of God's love.

According to popular evolutionary thought, altruistic behaviors are a matter of the survival instincts of the species. If I save someone, then some day they may save me.

Then again, altruism can mask other more nefarious motives: helping an elderly lady across the street may be a simple way of stealing her purse. The rescue of a person from a burning building may involve a quick stop at the jewelry chest.

An altruist might argue, "I've given vast sums to help those in need, what more do you want?!"

A religious zealot might say, "I've done all the things that religious law requires."

But God might reply, "The one thing I require, is found only in me. I want you to show *my* love by pouring out the love I give you. My love should pour out from your whole being--your heart, your soul, your mind and your strength. Follow my example of love and give me glory, just as Christ did by giving himself up for you on the cross" (Ephesians 5:1-2).

Just because the world does not quickly (or ever) unite with us in God's love, does not erase what mankind was created *for*. What it means is that we, tragically, have a world full of people separated from God who are in broken, cold, hurting, impersonal and threatening relationships with God and others.

God does not stand idly by. God works to fill the hearts of all his children with love. When we are born of the Spirit as children of God, we are washed, cleaned and filled to overflowing with love.

When we understand and live according to our design and purpose, we find our one true family in those who are united with us in love.

We are family, growing and building in love as a community. Our faith expresses itself in love.

Under God, we are united by love over works. We are united by love over blood lines. We are united by love over blaming others for the way we act.

Our *me* becomes *we.*

We become true family.

Forever.

DOCTRINE MATTERS
BUT LOVE MATTERS MORE

After all the talk about love, it all can fade and disappear in the mire of distraction and deception. We tend to be gullible, vulnerable to suggestion, easily distracted like sheep who wander off, ignorant of danger.

One dangerous distraction for Christians, is the pursuit of doctrinal unity as the highest priority over and above love. I believe doctrine is important. But love matters more. Here's why.

Developing doctrine based on Scripture necessarily involves interpretation. Although every church claims a Spirit-wrought interpretation of the God's Word, every interpretation obviously can't be right because our conclusions differ and conflict. It requires healthy humility to admit that interpretation by our theologians and teachers is inherently fallible.

I have learned this lesson the hard way. On the world Christian front, I have friends in Christ who claim that we can and must unify around human doctrine *at any cost.*

The problem is, when we try to create a definitive list of essential doctrines, we get frustrated. We can't agree on the number and the details. It's a terrible thing when the pursuit of doctrinal correctness turns to disunity, disharmony, judging and even damning each other.

Our prideful divisions, the banners we wave to support our causes, the finger pointing and the condemnation we wield to defend what we insist is the correct version of absolute truth, are an ugly blight on Christianity. The heart of the Church is portrayed as judgmental, intolerant, and divided.

The ecumenical church movement has valiantly tried for a century to achieve unity and harmony within the church of Christ. So far it hasn't worked. I believe the movement is innately flawed because the final chosen path to harmony and unity is agreement and/or compromise in doctrine.

Divisions among God's people are not easily (or ever) resolved when doctrinal unity is the only path to get there.

Paul, in his letter to the Ephesians, warned that we need to avoid being "tossed and blown here and there by every wind of teaching," and warned against people who are crafty and smart, who may deceive us by their teachings (Ephesians 4:14).

God has not locked down our basic human creativity, imagination or interpretation. We can make discoveries. We can make mistakes. We can err.

God has not poured out a perfect interpretation of the Bible into the minds of all of humanity so that we reach perfect understanding and agreement.

If that would be the case, the apostles of Christ certainly would have been unified by their doctrinal interpretation—yet the pages of the Bible show sharp disputes and disagreement among Jesus' disciples. Even with Jesus himself.

Our prideful pursuit and protection of doctrine *causes* divisions, and at times, outright war, crusades, and condemnations. At our worst, we look like children of a different father. Fixating on reaching doctrinal unity in the Church is an innately unstable endeavor, doing little to stem the tide of Christian divisions still forming today.

In bright contrast, Paul struggled with the same thoughts and advocated a different direction in his inspired conclusion:

> My goal is that they may be encouraged in heart
> and united in love. (Colossians 2:2a)

I, like Paul, have a tenacious belief that God's love has the power to unify. As mentioned before, Jesus' own disciples wrestled with interpretation and agreement in doctrine while they were with Jesus and long after he ascended into heaven. Yet they were united in love. God's love in Christ bound their hearts together.

In the end, I think we would find that if churches would join together in pouring out God's love as he intended, we would progress toward unity.

I'm not advocating doctrinal irresponsibility and lawlessness. If we say that love discards the Law, we have strayed far from the Biblical teaching on love. True love defines, summarizes and ultimately fulfills the Law.

Paul taught:

> Love is the fulfillment of the Law.
> (Romans 13:10b)

> Let no debt remain outstanding, except the
> continuing debt to love one another, for
> whoever loves others has fulfilled the Law.
> (Romans 13:8)

It all goes wrong when our pursuit of our decided interpretation of doctrine supersedes humble listening and meditating on God's Word.

Given our sinfulness, we can sell our souls to uninspired interpretations, translations, rule-making, posturing, proof-texting, and defending by shunning and damning others. The divided and judgmental state of many in the organized church today is evidence of the problem. We are like a symphony gone amok. And people are fleeing.

Paul saw potential unity in love. He understood the importance of the commands of Christ which tell us what church is supposed to be like.

Here is one of his most important descriptions. I use this in my discussions and teaching about love as part of the vision for the future church:

> Therefore, as God's chosen people, holy and dearly loved, clothe yourselves with compassion, kindness, humility, gentleness and patience. Bear with each other and forgive one another if any of you has a grievance against someone. Forgive as the Lord forgave you. And over all these virtues put on *love, which binds them all together in perfect unity.* (Colossians 3:12-14, emphasis mine)

Put on love is different from *put on doctrine.*

Try a little exercise. Take these phrases from Paul's famous "love chapter" in his first letter to the Corinthians chapter 13. Change the word *love* in the first line to the word *doctrine* and see if it works.

Love Is...

- Patient, kind
- Not envious, boastful, proud
- Not self-seeking
- Not easily angered
- Does not delight in evil
- Rejoices in the truth
- Always protects
- Always trusts
- Always hopes
- Never fails

THE KITCHEN TABLE

People are powerful observers. Eve observed that the fruit of the Tree of the Knowledge of Good and Evil in God's garden looked good to eat and had desirable benefits. With the evil coaxing of the devil, her observations went in the wrong direction. She took some of the fruit for herself and Adam. He ate the fruit she served up at their family's kitchen table.

It did not work out so well.

As parents and guardians, we attempt to provide the proper interpretation of life for our children at the kitchen table. What follows is a basic principle. What gets served up at the kitchen table becomes part of who we are and transfers to our behaviors elsewhere.

This is the case in church as well. What is learned at the kitchen table in our local church gatherings becomes part of us and affects our behaviors elsewhere. For better or worse, our tables at home reflect what we learn *at table* in church.

Emerging generations are increasingly sensitive to people's relationships within organizations. They hear the noise.

What concerns me is that the world is losing its healthy places to learn about relationships—the top two, church and family, are struggling because of

- More broken families

- More divorce

- More abuse

- More betrayal

- More bullying

- More selfishness

- More seeking escape

- More temptations

- More drug abuse

- More depression

- More godlessness

Families reflect, or mirror, their local churches. They want authentic personal relationships, but need leaders and healthy activities to move them forward. If our church family struggles to teach and practice love for one another when we gather, our families will tend to mirror the same thing.

God changes our world through his love. He has the power to change the minds and hearts of those who turn away from God and Christianity. He also has the power to change the relationships we have as brothers and sisters in Christ in our homes, schools, and churches. Our world desperately needs his love.

The good news is, God provides what we need.

3
THE MESSIAH
LOVE IN PERSON

In God's perfect timing, Jesus Christ appeared on the world stage. Angels, shepherds, and wise men celebrated his birth. Centuries-old prophecies about the coming of the Messiah, prepared the Jews to welcome him and listen to him. His message would change the world.

Out of love, God the Father sent his son, Jesus, into the world in order to save the world through him (John 3:16-17).

The disciples walked with Jesus, talked with him, and watched him give up his life on a cross. To their shock and amazement, his death wasn't the end. They saw him after God raised him from the dead, and they witnessed his ascension into heaven.

Jesus was and is the perfect image of God's love. He is a new testament to God's love. God displayed his love for the world to see, in and through his Son.

God's goal is to draw all people near and far into new life under him in love. Christ is the living demonstration of God's love poured out for us. All those who are under God in Christ are united in love through the power of his Spirit.

As you follow the ministry of Jesus recorded in the gospel writings, there was a special teaching moment when Jesus revealed his purpose while he was with his disciples. That moment came on the night before his crucifixion.

THE NIGHT OF THE COMMAND

More than any other narrative in the Bible, the account of the night before Christ's crucifixion in John 13:1-20 brings to the forefront Jesus' teaching on love for one another.

On that night, Jesus prepared his disciples for what was to come. His suffering and death loomed on the horizon. He took a towel and water, and patiently washed his disciple's feet. Then he explained what he wanted his disciples to do in the future.

During his demonstration, Jesus' closest disciple, Peter, resisted Jesus' effort to wash his feet.

Peter quickly changed his mind when Jesus said:

> Unless I wash you, you have no part with me.
> (John 13:8b)

Jesus concluded his demonstration for his disciples with the following instruction:

> Now that I, your Lord and Teacher, have washed
> your feet, you also should wash one another's
> feet. I have set you an example that you should do
> as I have done for you.
> (John 13:14-15)

What did the foot washing illustrate? Jesus provided an example as a backdrop for this parting directive:

> A new command I give you: Love one another. As I
> have loved you, so you must love one another. By
> this everyone will know that you are my disciples,
> if you love one another.
> (John 13:34-35)

Love one another is a mark of the disciple and a *new* command. Yet, it sure sounds old to me—as old as that verse in Leviticus commanding love for our neighbor.

On the other hand, it sounds new because it came from the lips of the Messiah himself. This new command was given to the disciples at the crux of Christ's work on earth.

37

Jesus gave his disciples this new command with a purpose. This command was designated by Jesus as the distinguishing mark of his followers.

Paul understood this and it showed in his preaching and teaching long after Christ ascended:

> Walk in the way of love, just as Christ loved us and gave himself up for us... (Ephesians 5:2a, emphasis mine)

In his beautiful illustration of the Vine and Branches in John 15, Jesus made the point that our connection with him is essential to bearing fruit. Jesus explained that bearing the fruit of love is the mark of a disciple:

> This is to my Father's glory, that you bear much fruit, showing yourselves to be my disciples. As the Father has loved me, so have I loved you. Now remain in my love. If you keep my commands, you will remain in my love, just as I have kept my Father's commands and remain in his love...My command is this: Love each other as I have loved you. (John 15:8-10,12)

Jesus taught the primacy of love in our relationships with God and each other. He put it this way:

> 'Love the LORD your God with all your heart and with all your soul and with all your mind.' This is the first and greatest commandment.
> And the second is like it: 'Love your neighbor as yourself.' (Matthew 22:37-39)

Jesus indicated just how inclusive these commands were:

> All the Law and prophets hang on these two commands. (Matthew 22:40)

Jesus was referring to the original commands, mentioned in the last chapter, from Deuteronomy 6:5 and Leviticus 19:18b given by God through Moses. These essential commands were ingrained in the Jewish teachings, identity and community. You can see this, for example, in Jesus' dialog with a Jewish legal expert:

> On one occasion an expert in the Law stood up to test Jesus. "Teacher," he asked, "what must I do to inherit eternal life?"
>
> "What is written in the Law?" he replied. "How do you read it?"
>
> He answered, "'Love the Lord your God with all your heart and with all your soul and with all your strength and with all your mind'; and, 'Love your neighbor as yourself.'"
>
> "You have answered correctly," Jesus replied. "Do this and you will live."
>
> (Luke 10:25-28)

According to Jesus, love describes our life, as commanded in the Law and the prophets. God created and designed us to love.

When we love God and each other, we show glimpses of the God and Father who made us, just like Jesus did.

Our children are supposed to learn this as well. We are to talk about this when we get up in the morning, when we sit at the kitchen table, and when we walk along the road (Deuteronomy 6:6-7).

Jesus confirmed and personalized the Mosaic command to love God and our neighbor through his messianic teaching. His life and death was an illustration of God's love *in person*. Jesus illustrated God's love for his disciples when he washed their feet. Jesus poured out God's love when he suffered and died on the cross for us.

Jesus demonstrated God's love for us when he forgave us, and gave us new life in his name. What a beautiful movement in the symphony of God.

THE PAST INFORMS THE PRESENT

I was called to serve as pastor in a church that is almost as old as the state of Wisconsin. When we celebrated our 150th anniversary, I looked through the old, dusty documents written at the inception of our church. The documents spelled out the purpose of our church. One hundred fifty years later, our old church still states the same purpose.

Our church was shaped by its past. The buildings changed. The people changed. The landscape changed. Yet, established in the past, our purpose did not change.

Like the great commandments of old, our church's statements of conviction were hanging pegs for our Christian community that continued far beyond the first few generations.

Jesus repeatedly quoted from the past to address questions in the present. In the same way, God's eternal Word from the past shapes what we think and believe today.

Love underlies the entire Biblical narrative. It surprised me the first time I realized that the common Biblical words *grace, faith, believe,* and *obey* are not used to summarize the Law and the Prophets in the Old Testament. This is not an accident. *Love* is a powerful and adequate summary.

The disciples got it. For example, John in his later writings connected Christ's ministry at the beginning, to loving one another:

> This is the message you heard from the beginning: We should love one another. (1 John 3:11)

> I am not writing you a new command but one we have had from the beginning. I ask that we love one another. (2 John 1:5)

> [Jesus] has given us this command: Anyone who loves God must also love their brother and sister. (1 John 4:21)

In the expanding early Christian Church, Paul's letters to the Romans and Galatians sound the same as the teachings of Christ:

> The commandments, "You shall not commit adultery," "You shall not murder," "You shall not steal," "You shall not covet," and whatever other command there may be, are summed up in this one command: "Love your neighbor as yourself." (Romans 13:9)

> For the entire Law is fulfilled in keeping this one command: "Love your neighbor as yourself." (Galatians 5:14)

Everything falls under love. Think of it this way. Faith matters, but love matters more. Truth matters, but love matters more. Grace matters, but love matters more.

Loving one another was the defining mark of the disciples in obedience to the original great commandments and Jesus' new command (John 13:35). God's love for believers was shown in person through Christ for us to see and imitate. He showed us the way things are supposed to be.

From the beginning of the Christian Church, the most prominent feature of local church gatherings was supposed to be love for God and others.

Love is comprehensive. What Jesus taught his disciples about love is central to the understanding of the Gospel and all the related doctrines in Scripture including salvation and sanctified living. His apostles taught this well, providing invaluable instruction for the people they were inspired to teach. Here are a few quotes.

John wrote:

> Whoever does not love does not know God, because God is love. (1 John 4:8)

> Whoever claims to love God yet hates a brother or sister is a liar. For whoever does not love their brother and sister, whom they have seen, cannot love God, whom they have not seen. (1 John 4:20)

> We know that we have passed from death to life, because we love each other. Anyone who does not love remains in death. (1 John 3:14)

> If anyone has material possessions and sees a brother or sister in need but has no pity on them, how can the love of God be in that person? (1 John 3:17)

Paul wrote:

> If I have the gift of prophecy and can fathom all mysteries and all knowledge, and if I have a faith that can move mountains, but do not have love, I am nothing. (1 Corinthians 13:2)

Be devoted to one another in love.

(Romans 12:10a)

Be completely humble and gentle; be patient,

bearing with one another in love.

(Ephesians 4:2)

Peter wrote:

Be like-minded, be sympathetic, love one

another... (1 Peter 3:8a)

MORE THAN A FEELING

If you like language and word studies, you might want to study the New Testament words for different types of love in Greek. There are several words for specific kinds of love. Although it is interesting, what is lost or gained in translation does not change the most basic teachings about love.

The message of God's love is universal and timeless. It spans the Old and New Testaments. The Gospel message, or Word of love from God, is about God, and *is* God from the beginning (John 1:1-2). That is why the famous Gospel-in-a-nutshell starts like this:

God so loved the world... (John 3:16a)

Love is more than a feeling. This is very important to understand. In our cultural context, we primarily think of love as affection. Jesus' command to love others is not a command to *feel* loving feelings. Although we might.

Rather, it is a command to *overflow* with love from our hearts, whether we feel like it or not. God's love shows itself in commitment, sacrifice and light.

Loving feelings do not always accompany true love. There will be times when we grit our teeth and pour out God's love in spite of our feelings at the moment.

Jesus set the supreme example when he faced pain, suffering and death for us.

Love is more than an emotion created by chemicals in the body. It comes from outside of us, rather than from the inside. It is sourced in the heart of God who pours out love for us, in us, and through us by his Spirit. God's love flows through us in love toward God and others (Galatians 5:6b). As God's love pours out of us in loving actions, people encounter God's love, sometimes in spite of our personal feelings.

Nowhere is this taught more clearly than in the teachings of Jesus about loving our enemies:

> But to you who are listening I say: Love your enemies, do good to those who hate you, bless those who curse you, pray for those who mistreat you. (Luke 6:27-28)

> Love your enemies, do good to them, and lend to them without expecting to get anything back. Then your reward will be great, and you will be children of the Most High, because he is kind to the ungrateful and wicked. Be merciful, just as your Father is merciful. (Luke 6:35-36)

Paul told the church in Rome how to treat those they may not like:

> Live in harmony with one another. Do not be proud, but be willing to associate with people of low position. Do not be conceited.
> (Romans 12:16)

This is tough, especially if emotions typically drive our actions. Could I encounter someone in my family, church or small group that I know hates me, and yet still love them? If love is all about God's love flowing through me, what may seem impossible becomes possible. That's life changing for our daily lives.

Jesus expressed the whole spectrum of emotion toward others: anger, joy, compassion, grief, and sadness. His love, however, was not dependent on those feelings. His love came from the heart of God the Father and was demonstrated in his submissive and humble actions.

We saw this most clearly in his betrayal, suffering, and death. He shared the cup with Judas. He prayed for his persecutors. He loved and gave up his life for his enemies, despite of how he must have felt.

Reflect for a moment:

- How well do we love others?
- Is this the kind of love we portray when we gather together as God's people?
- Is our love only poured out when we feel like it?

COUNSEL TO LOVE

When anger and tensions arise, loving feelings quickly disappear. I teach this principle in marriage counseling. True love wins, over and above our feelings.

Christian love is sourced in God's love flowing into our hearts, not our momentary and fleeting feelings. God expects and commands us to flow with love toward one another in our words and actions.

Our love is a result of God's love in Christ for us, to us, in us, and through us.

When struggling couples begin to trust in God's love and act lovingly despite their feelings, it helps them navigate through the waters of a troubled marriage.

This is true in our relationship with God as well. Our feelings of love for God may be hot or tepid at any given moment. True love comes from God, and the love of God prevails when we pour out love toward each other despite our feelings. He commands us to act according to who we are created and redeemed to be. We are to love God and others with our whole being.

Christian parents can benefit from understanding this. Our children sometimes act in love only when they feel like it. This is because the part of their brain that governs their actions has yet to mature. It is a major battle for many parents, reaching its peak in the chaotic teenage years.

As parents, we can't make our child *feel* a certain way. Instead, we ask that they commit to obey us out of love. Separate from their feelings. After all, we believe God has poured out his love in them and is working in their hearts to pour out love toward us as parents. When we see it, we affirm it. This teaching requires consistency, affirmation, and repetition especially through the years of adolescent development.

We do what's right based on our faith versus our feelings. This can be taught in a variety of situations—for instance, in a child's decision to obey or disobey. Our feelings about things can change if we think about it first and let our beliefs inform our reactions—similar to the practice of counting to ten before reacting.

LOVE AND LIVE LIKE JESUS

When love pours into us from the heart of God, it saturates our whole being, like rushing water in a river. It fills and cleans our hearts. It washes away the dirt and stain. It makes its way into the remote corners of our minds. It saturates our thoughts and consciences.

It settles in our souls.

Jesus was love *in person*. He showed us how a person can be filled with the Holy Spirit and love. We are followers of his example in word and deed.

John explained we live like Christ:

> This is how love is made complete among us so that we will have confidence on the day of judgment: In this world we are like Jesus.
> (1 John 4:17)

Paul wrote that we are to love like Christ:

> Christ's love compels us, because we are convinced that one died for all, and therefore all died. And he died for all, that those who live should no longer live for themselves but for him who died for them and was raised again.
> (2 Corinthians 5:14-15)

Jesus tied self-sacrifice to love:

> Whoever wants to be my disciple must deny themselves and take up their cross daily and follow me. (Luke 9:23)

> Greater love has no one than this: to lay down one's life for one's friends. (John 15:13)

John connected Christ's sacrifice to us:

> This is how we know what love is: Jesus Christ laid down his life for us. And we ought to lay down our lives for our brothers and sisters. (1 John 3:16)

LOVE IS A LIGHT

The light of God's love is intended to shine in the whole world—transforming our relationships with God and one another. I love some of the catchy songs and hymns that have been written about shining our light in this dark world. Jesus teaches in Matthew that the light we shine is our *good deeds*. The only true source of good deeds is love which ultimately glorifies the Father.

He said:

> You are the light of the world. A town built on a hill cannot be hidden. Neither do people light a lamp and put it under a bowl. Instead they put it on its stand, and it gives light to everyone in the house. In the same way, let your light shine before others, that they may see your good deeds and glorify your Father in heaven. (Matthew 5:14-16)

This is important to the success or failure of our Christian witness.

Today, people who observe us in our gatherings have their relational antennas up. In other words, they are very sensitive when observing loving or unloving behavior in our relationships as a Christian family. They are affected positively or negatively by how we treat each other.

Relationships filled with God's love are dynamic, relatable and real. We know that blood alone does not define family—love does. We don't expect perfection, but we want to see the evidence of love. We hope we might somehow love one another in the end.

We are naturally and spiritually drawn to observing and experiencing broken relationships transformed and redeemed by God in love and forgiveness. It is world-changing.

Jesus made a point about his real spiritual family when he said:

> 'Who is my mother, and who are my
> brothers?' Pointing to his disciples, he said, 'Here
> are my mother and my brothers. For whoever
> does the will of my Father in heaven is my brother
> and sister and mother.'
> (Matthew 12:48b-50)

Jesus summarized the will of the Father by identifying the two great commandments—love God and love your neighbor. Christian family is made up of those who live together in love from the heart of God. We are united as family based on love. The family of God is committed to loving God and others with all our hearts, just as Christ did.

People can tell when we get it right. Jesus used relatable illustrations of love all the time, both from real life and through parables.

Here are a few examples from his ministry:

- The king who forgives the huge debt of his servant (Matthew 18:21-35).

- The Father who welcomes the prodigal son (Luke 15:11-32).

51

- The return of the one of ten healed lepers, to express love and thanks to God and Christ (Luke 17:11-19).

- The good Samaritan who helped the man who was robbed (Luke 10:25-37).

- The separation of the sheep and goats based on acts of love toward others (Matthew 25:31-46).

We recognize love when we see it. Others can see it too. God's banner waving over us is love. He wants us to see his love and believe. That is why he put his Son, Jesus Christ, on the cross. That is why he fills us with his love. In turn, we love him and one another. This is our identifying mark as disciples. We wave the banner of God's love when we love.

In the future, we definitely can improve what we do in our local church gatherings. A trickle of love for others isn't good enough. We need a new way to engage everyone in loving one another—pouring out love the way God intended. We need a change.

Brace yourself.

Section 2

Listen Pray Care

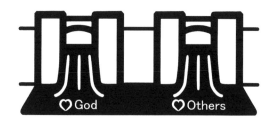

4
THE METHOD
LISTEN PRAY CARE

Christian relationships are like a dam on the river of love with two release gates. Gate number one releases *love for God*. Gate number two releases *love for one another*. Both come from the same Source and bring a flow of honor and worship to God. In Scripture, love for one another is part of our love and worship of God (Ephesians 5:1-2; Hebrews 6:10).

In today's Christian church gatherings, we generously and consistently open gate number one and the result is impressive—love pours out toward God in beautiful expressions of words, music and actions.

Opening gate number two, the subject of this book, is a different matter. In many gatherings, it is barely opened. Especially in our largest gatherings. Not everyone is loved, and not everyone loves. The result is an unimpressive trickle of love for others.

Most of us know *why* we need to love one another, but we don't know exactly how to make that happen. I have felt for a long time that we need a consistent way to generously release God's love in our relationships with others in our gatherings. We need a method of raising high gate number two.

I made a trip to South Dakota during the Missouri River flood of 2011, which was caused by record rain and snow. I visited the Fort Randall Dam which was breaking all water-release records that summer. I was floored by the powerful sound of the rushing water. It was jaw-dropping. I could hear the roar miles away from the dam. When I arrived at the dam itself...now, *that* was an impressive experience. The earth shook. It was deafening. I was stunned.

Now, think for a moment. How does our love for one another *sound*? Imagine the sound of a Christian church family engaged in sharing and praying for each other. It would be a beautiful sound indeed. Yet, is that what we do? Is that something we *could* do?

The reputation of Christianity is at the forefront of this question. We are being observed with detached interest by relationally sensitive people in our emerging generations. When God's love flows between us, it is a spiritually impressive display of love in a world in need of love. God created us to show it. His Spirit prepares us for it. People will be drawn to it.

OUR CURRENT METHODS DON'T WORK

It takes some skill to diagnose what's wrong with something. When my car starts to break down, I hear strange noises and feel shudders in the steering wheel, but that doesn't mean I know what's wrong or how to fix it.

Getting a symphony to play together takes a leader, who is a musical mechanic of sorts, to analyze the problems and get things in working order. In order to get a symphony of relationships to flow with the love of God, it takes specific, deliberate and intentional actions, led by people who know what they are doing. Our leaders help us hear the command of God, submit to our purpose, and grow and mature in loving one another.

We are like a speed boat preparing for launch. Shallow waters provide the opportunity to load our boat and prepare for deeper water. As a matter of course, when we leave the shallows, our boat is able to fulfill its purpose as a *speed* boat.

Our Christian gatherings are designed for speed runs. We are designed to do more than sit in shallow water relationships. We are created to be loved by God and to love others with all he's given us. Running fast and smooth in open waters.

Just being in the water is not enough.

Back in the 1990's, I was introduced to a new approach to Christian ministry that encouraged the creation of cell groups. The intent was to increase relational intimacy through proximity, familiarity, and interaction, which is inherently difficult in larger gatherings. The saying I heard from conversations was, *we grow smaller as we grow larger.*

Small groups worked. They increased intimacy in our relationships. Unfortunately, in contrast to running fast, it still was mostly slow going in shallow waters. Small groups puttered along in selective and shallow love for one another, because they were generally mirroring our large groups. Something else was needed in addition to intimacy.

Here is an example of the method of loving one another in traditional Christian gatherings.

I label it the *Leader Loves* method.

The *Leader Loves* method is limited because a single person is tasked with loving the whole group. Notice how people are left out.

Smaller groups don't necessarily eliminate the problem. They can simply be smaller versions of our larger groups when using the *Leader Loves* method.

Another method of loving one another in our gatherings is the *Moved by the Spirit* method. Waiting for what feels like the right time, group members are spontaneously inspired by the Spirit to love on someone.

In the end, there is a similar, selective result. Some are loved. Some are not.

These methods aren't *wrong*, they just aren't very effective. We are speed boats slowly motoring around in shallow water. In these models, the floodgate is only open for the leader or the inspired. Words and good intentions are not the same as showing love in our actions with everyone involved.

We need to humbly admit that we struggle to consistently love everyone. I believe this can change.

Here are a few reasons why change may be difficult:

- We don't have a basic way to describe what it means to love one another that is easy to understand and remember.

- We are not intentional or deliberate about engaging each and every person in love for one another.

- We get hung up on faith alone, sometimes to the exclusion of love.

- The motive to change is weak. We have low expectations. We get *some* results. Our current methods do result in occasional love for one another, masking the urgency of the problem.

- Some adhere to the myth that loving others is bad because it takes our focus off of God when we gather for worship. Loving one another is not correctly understood as love flowing from the heart of God which brings glory and worship back to God. This myth contradicts the connection between our love for others and our love for God as revealed in Hebrews 6:10:

  God is not unjust; he will not forget your work and
  the love you have shown him as you have helped
  his people and continue to help them.

I am proposing a commitment to Jesus' relational strategy, which is the most effective. His vision for gatherings of his followers is that *each person* shows love to others. Each person washes feet.

It's simple. God loves each person in Christ. Each person is filled with his love. Each person loves. Each person is loved.

Paul clearly taught this:

> From [Christ] the whole body, joined and held together by every supporting ligament, grows and builds itself up in love, *as each part does its work.* (Ephesians 4:16, emphasis mine)

What does this mean for us? This means in the future we will have to teach and train the whole Church on earth how to actively love one another in our gatherings. This includes: parents, children, youth, seniors, young adults, and our leaders—pastors, counselors, elders, youth leaders, educators, coaches.

We are all part of it.

This is the core of living as children of God—everyone learns, grows, and matures in practicing love for one another when we gather.

To get started, we need a simple way of teaching the basics of loving one another.

CREATING THE METHOD

Zeroing in on a specific way of describing love for one another was a long, seven-year process. In my research and discussions with close friends, I was unable to find an existing method of loving one another that involved everyone and would work in regular large gatherings.

The method needed to be:

- Broad enough to cover the basics.

- Understandable and memorable.

- Simple enough for children.

In designing a new way to do this, I drew from the success of parents and teachers who created a way to help our children understand and remember what to do in potentially dangerous situations—specifically, if their clothes catch fire or when they cross the street or railroad tracks. For children, it needs to be simple in addition to being effective.

In the case of clothes catching fire, children are taught Stop, Drop, and Roll. Think about how simple this is.

As much as there are more complicated ways of putting out flames, such as using fire extinguishers or finding a pool or lake to jump in, this method is one of the least complicated ways of doing it.

While a skilled gymnast may be able to do fancy rolls, flips and tumbles, it is not required. A young child can simply Stop, Drop, and Roll!

Parents understand the dire importance of teaching their children how to safely cross the street or railroad tracks.

In my home town, we have railroad tracks that run through the center of town. Sadly, years back, several children were killed at a railroad crossing. Our community decided to construct some attractive signs near the tracks to remind children of the basics of safe crossing.

Stop, Look, and Listen is simple, and easy to understand and remember for children. This is exactly what I was seeking—a way to teach the basics to people of any age who are learning to love one another.

I asked myself, "If we are challenged by Christ to love someone, what are the three things every Christian should do?" The goal was a solution that would be simple and effective in a wide variety of settings.

The final result was *Listen Pray Care*™, a new relational strategy that breaks down loving one another into three simple actions that are easy to understand and remember.

The three actions of loving one another are:

- *Listen*—listening to understand.
- *Pray*—trusting God to take care of the things that matter.
- *Care*—helping and giving sacrificially.

Listen Pray Care™ helps us be specific about what we mean by *loving one another*. Our children, or anyone we may be leading and training, can quickly learn and remember what we have taught them.

Listen Pray Care allows us to easily evaluate our relationships in our gatherings by asking: "Were you listened to, prayed for, and cared for?" And, "Did you get a chance to listen, pray, and care for others?"

- ☑ *Listen*
- ☑ *Pray*
- ☑ *Care*

Jesus envisioned gatherings in His name to be a place where everyone is loved, and everyone loves to the glory of God the Father. As we *Listen Pray Care*, everyone is listened to, prayed for, cared for and everyone listens, prays and cares.

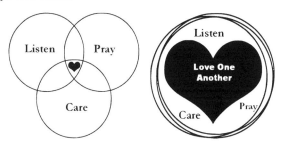

It is a lifetime process. As we listen, pray, and care, our love for one another grows and matures.

Since God's love is meant to pour out from us, we should expect to love one another whenever and wherever we gather together. Jesus commanded it. Floodgate number two should be wide open. People will be able to see and hear the sound of listening, praying and caring in our gatherings.

So, how do we start this in a large organization like a church? Consider working in stages. You may begin teaching and practicing *Listen Pray Care* in casual interactions with others. Then move to smaller group settings.

When you are ready, you may incorporate *Listen Pray Care* into Sunday gatherings as an essential part of the worship service.

5
LISTEN
LISTENING TO UNDERSTAND

Let's take a closer look at the three components of *Listen Pray Care*.

When practicing *Listen Pray Care*, our love for one another starts with *Listen*. *Listen* lays the groundwork for prayers that are specific and care that is effective. When we listen to each other, we give our attention to understanding other's needs, to better pray and care for them.

As God's love pours in our hearts and through us to others, we open ourselves to the lives of others by listening.

Loving human relationships are built on deep communication. It is a fact of life. *Listen* goes beyond physically hearing words—we *listen to understand.*

As a pastoral counselor, I spend a lot of time listening to understand and helping people learn to do the same to improve their relationships with others. We act in love when we listen.

One of each person's deepest needs is *to be understood.* I encounter this every day in youth work and my own experience raising teens. Teens want to be understood. Listening to understand takes work—a lot of work.

One of the most common complaints I hear from teens is: "My parents don't listen to me." Although it literally can be true, the underlying message almost always is: "My parents don't understand me."

Listening to understand involves trying to see what the person is communicating. As you listen, use your imagination and develop a picture of their need, struggle, or celebration. You'll know you are on the right path if after listening you say, "Oh, I see!"

You really can't judge a book by its cover. People are the same way. We rarely know what is going on inside a person by examining them from the outside. I suppose we could know some of the general needs of someone who is literally stuck in the mud, but not what they are feeling, thinking, and struggling with inside.

Suppose a person has a cut on their face, a house smashed by a tornado, or a broken leg. Our best guesses of what they need are only guesses. By listening to understand, we may find that in these tragic circumstances people are worried about different things than the obvious.

For example, they may be worried about losing their income, what people will think, if their family is OK, or what will happen if their cousin dies. When we listen, we may find that people are thankful for *just* a broken leg or a cut on the face. Or that the tornado only hit their house and not their child's house a block away.

In order to love people in effective and meaningful ways, we need a window into their thoughts and feelings. *Listen* provides a window into their hearts and souls, giving us pictures we can use for specific prayer and effective care—the next two actions in LPC.

Listen Tips

- **Make sure you listen**—it is impossible to talk and fully engage in listening at the same time.

- **Listen to understand**—not to give answers, counsel or correct what a person is saying.

- **Listen for *ups* and *downs***—this is a simple way of describing things we are thankful for and things we need to entrust to God.

- **"See" what they are going through**—picture it, imagine it, and put yourself in their shoes.

- **See things from the other person's perspective**—first.

- **Give feedback**—show you understand what was said.

- **Listen with love and respect**—this is part of loving one another.

- **Follow Paul's advice**—"In humility value others above yourselves, not looking to your own interests but each of you to the interests of others" (Philippians 2:3b-4), and, "Be quick to listen and slow to speak" (James 1:19b).

- **Be patient**—give people time to express their thoughts and feelings completely.

- **Show love, patience and forgiveness for difficult people**—follow Christ's example.

6
PRAY
TRUST AND THANKS

After *Listen*, we engage in *Pray*—the second action in *Listen Pray Care*. *Pray* is turning our attention and trust to God and being thankful. Our relationship with our neighbor is inextricably linked to our relationship with God. People who *Pray*, walk with God. People who walk with God, walk in love.

TRUST AND THANKS

Keep prayer simple. *Pray* is basically two things: trust and thanks. This second step of *Listen Pray Care* is a response to the things learned in the first step—Listen. We listen for things people need to entrust to God and things they are grateful for. We then lift those things to God in prayer.

Thanks includes:

- Worship of God for his greatness.

- Gratitude for his love and provision.

- Generously offering ourselves to God's future work through us.

Trust includes:

- Entrusting God with the things that matter.

- Laying burdens at his feet.

- Giving problems beyond our control to God.

- Confessing we need his mercy and love.

- Asking God for his provision.

- Finding Sabbath rest for our souls in God.

Pray is an exercise of trusting our heavenly Father to take care of all the things that matter and thanking him when he does. *Pray* puts into words the things we feel and believe in our hearts. *Pray* results from God's love filling our hearts.

Pray reflects our position of faith in God's grace and mercy through Jesus Christ in all circumstances. It benefits our mind, spirit, and soul. Our prayers also benefit those who pray with us.

In prayer, we actively set our hearts and minds on God and his provision.

Paul talked about it this way:

> Set your minds on things above, not on earthly
> things. (Colossians 3:2)

With our minds fixed on things above, *Pray* is part of everything we do:

> And whatever you do, whether in word or deed, do
> it all in the name of the Lord Jesus, giving
> thanks to God the Father through him.
> (Colossians 3:17)

Here is an example of listening to a child's heart and responding with prayer:

> "When is daddy coming home, Mommy?"
>
> "That's a good question, honey. Come here and
> let's pray about that... Dear God, wherever Daddy
> is, be with him. Keep him safe. And bring him
> home to us soon. In Jesus' name we pray, Amen."

With our minds and hearts set on God, we reestablish our position of trust in God *together as a spiritual family.* We deeply love one another when we *Pray.*

73

We are strong in our relationship with God, tied and bound together as believers in love.

THE RIGHT PERSPECTIVE

We have a frightfully small window to view the world around us. I use the word *frightfully* to indicate the fear, almost panic, that accompanies being unable to see what is happening around us, especially when we feel something scary is chasing us.

We reassure ourselves that we are going to be OK, but we feel the harsh realities of life lurking just around the corner. They threaten our confidence in the little we can see.

With maturity comes perspective. At first, children are excellent observers, but poor interpreters. The older we get, the better we become at interpreting what to pray for and how to pray for it. We get better at turning over the things we can't control. We have more experience with God's provision and finding rest for our souls.

We can use what we learn from God to better respond to the things we hear from our brothers and sisters as they share. We can't have and won't have solutions to many of the needs presented to us. We believe, however, that there is something we can and should do in response to what we learn from others when listening to them. We should *Pray*.

Pray is an act of humility.

We surrender our needs, thanksgivings and concerns to God. It is tied with our sacrificial giving as we offer our lives as living sacrifices in worship of God (Romans 12:1). We offer our prayers to God as a way of saying *in God we trust*. We live our lives *under* God.

Pray is an act of faith. *Pray* is an act of worship. *Pray* is an act of love. We essentially give over everything to God in respect and honor of his ultimate power and our dependence on him for everything. We trust we are going to be OK because God is in control of the things that matter.

The fact that we live, breathe, and act on our own is only an illusion. God is the source and provider of all things, including life and breath.

God helps us come to the realization that we are ultimately dependent on him for all things. God uses life's uncontrollable circumstances to steer us in the right direction—toward him. He works through our needs to develop greater trust in him.

When our knees are bent before God, we show on the outside, the inside truth that God is in control. As a result, when our listening reveals our neighbor's need to trust in God, we act and *Pray*.

The Bible is full of examples of God's family needing to trust him during difficult or tempting circumstances. The temptation of Eve clouded her perspective of whether or not to obey God's command (Genesis 3:1-6). Cain's anger clouded his perspective of whether or not he should kill his brother Abel (Genesis 4:4-7).

The Israelites lost perspective and grumbled and complained about their lives soon after God delivered them (Numbers 14:17). Elijah believed he was the only person left who was faithful to God (1 Kings 19:14,18). Peter thought it was time to fight the soldiers who came to arrest Jesus in the Garden of Gethsemane. But Jesus told him to put his sword away (John 18:10-11).

Thankfully, we have a great high priest—Jesus—who knows us just as we are, therefore we can pray to God with confidence:

> "Let us then approach God's throne of grace with confidence, so that we may receive mercy and find grace to help us in our time of need. (Hebrews 4:16)

Jesus told his disciples to ask the Father for whatever they needed:

> Very truly I tell you, my Father will give you whatever you ask in my name. (John 16:23b)

Here is a sample of Bible verses that show God designed us to pray as we live under him:

> And pray in the Spirit on all occasions with all kinds of prayers and requests. With this in mind, be alert and always keep on praying for all the Lord's people. (Ephesians 6:18)
>
> Pray continually. (1 Thessalonians 5:17)

Do not be anxious about anything, but in every situation, by prayer and petition, with thanksgiving, present your requests to God. (Philippians 4:6)

We ought always to thank God for you, brothers and sisters, and rightly so, because your faith is growing more and more, and the love all of you have for one another is increasing.
(1 Thessalonians 1:3)

Therefore confess your sins to each other and pray for each other so that you may be healed. The prayer of a righteous person is powerful and effective. (James 5:16)

SABBATH PRAYER

Pray has an amazing benefit. It is a way to find peace and rest in this life. Every time we turn things over to God, we have an opportunity to rest our hearts and souls. Taking on the needs of others by listening and caring can quickly become overwhelming.

Sharing our needs with others can be stressful too, causing us internal turmoil and unrest.

Paul wrote about the very real challenges he faced as a follower of Christ. Moved by the Spirit, he taught about about prayer and trust in God bringing rest and peace of mind and spirit:

> Do not be anxious about anything, but in every
> situation, by prayer and petition, with
> thanksgiving, present your requests to God. And
> the peace of God, which transcends all
> understanding, will guard your hearts and your
> minds in Christ Jesus. (Philippians 4:6-7)

God did not expect that we would take on the needs of others until we reach our breaking point. His plan was for us to rest. He expects us to lay down our burdens at his feet and be thankful for his blessings, acknowledging that he is the sole provider of all things good. In the process, we find rest for our souls.

It is also important that we do not make the task of loving others our work alone. If we practice giving over our burdens to God, how heavy is the burden that remains?

God does the work. He loves others through us. It is God's infinite love that fills us and empowers us, so we can take the relatively light burden that remains, and be assured that God will provide the strength, endurance and all that is needed for us to love as he loved us.

Traumatic events are tough. I have found it hard to rest in the middle of difficult situations. When there is time taken to pray, no matter how short, my mind and soul find rest in God. When we pray with someone, we mutually encourage each other to rest in God.

THE PRAYER OF A CHILD

Pray is intimidating when you feel self-conscious and inexperienced. God does not need our many words because he already knows what we need.

In prayer, we ask for help and express trust and dependence on God with all our hearts.

The prayer of a child is just as powerful and effective as that of an adult. Child-like prayers are simple and beautiful: "Dear God, I love you. Thank you for my food and for my family. Amen." or "God, help my sister. She is feeling sick. Please make her better. In Jesus' name I pray, Amen."

Using many words does not make our prayers better. Jesus commented on this very thing:

> And when you pray, do not keep on babbling like pagans, for they think they will be heard because of their many words. Do not be like them, for your Father knows what you need before you ask him.
> (Matthew 6:7-8)

When you give something to God's care, remember that there are an infinite number of words that could be used. The exact words, fancy words, or number of them make no difference to God.

Sometimes, the exquisitely crafted, formal, and lengthy prayers in our gatherings by our leaders intimidate us. We, understandably, say to ourselves, "I could never pray like that." It's probably true.

However, don't worry about *how* you pray. Pray simply and from the heart. Since child-like prayer is the standard, everyone can pray.

PRAY AND UNBELIEF

It is important to mention that we should not to force someone to pray. Faith as small as a mustard seed is all that is needed to pray.

However, if a person does not believe in God, they should not be forced to *Pray*. Acquaintances and guests may feel unready for prayer in *Listen Pray Care* (LPC). They should be given permission to pass when it is their turn to pray.

They still can benefit from the activities of LPC as people listen, pray, and care for them. Also, they can do their part and fully participate in the listening and caring activities of LPC.

Pray Tips

- **Remember the two parts of** *Pray*—trust and thanks.

- **Prayer is loving your neighbor**—your heart pours out God's love.

- **Remember the prayer of a child**—simple prayer is all that is needed.

- **Pray from your heart**—exact words are not important.

- **Do not force people to pray**—those who are not ready should not be required to pray.

- **Give things over to God**—especially things you can't control.

- **Pray with confidence**—God knows what matters in every situation. Pray like Jesus—*not my will, but yours be done.*

- **Find your peace and rest in God**—give your soul what it needs.

7
CARE
CARING IN LOVE

Care is the third action in *Listen Pray Care*. *Care* is God's love pouring out from us in selfless, sacrificial, Christ-like action toward the benefit of others. *Pray* is our vertical response to what we learn when we *Listen*. *Care* is our horizontal response. *Care* covers everything we might do to love our neighbor in response to listening to their needs. That covers a lot of territory.

In many cases, *Care* is easy to figure out. Try answering these questions:

- If someone is thirsty, what do you do?

- If someone is hungry, how do you help them?

- If someone is lonely and needs a visit, what might you do?

- If someone is grieving, how do you aid them?

- If someone is upset, how might you assist?

Ask your children these questions. Most young children can identify loving and caring responses right away.

GENEROSITY

Paul describes how generosity is part of *Care* in his second letter to the Corinthians:

> Remember this: Whoever sows sparingly will also reap sparingly, and whoever sows generously will also reap generously. Each of you should give what you have decided in your heart to give, not reluctantly or under compulsion, for God loves a cheerful giver. (2 Corinthians 9:6-7)

Notice the free and selfless nature of *Care*. It is a reflection of God's generous and selfless love.

Paul said it this way:

> God is able to bless you abundantly, so that in all
> things at all times, having all that you need, you
> will abound in every good work....You will be
> enriched in every way so that you can be generous
> on every occasion, and through us your
> generosity will result in thanksgiving to God.
> (2 Corinthians 9:8,11)

Paul continues by connecting *Care* to our witness and the praise of God:

> Others will praise God for the obedience that
> accompanies your confession of the gospel of
> Christ, and for your generosity in sharing with
> them and with everyone else.
> (2 Corinthians 9:13b)

To those who have much to give, Paul instructs:

> Command those who are rich in this present
> world not to be arrogant nor to put their hope in
> wealth, which is so uncertain, but to put their
> hope in God, who richly provides us with
> everything for our enjoyment. Command them to
> do good, to be rich in good deeds, and to be
> generous and willing to share.
> (1 Timothy 6:17-18)

Care is love in action—matching the words we say with the things we believe:

> If anyone has material possessions and sees a
> brother or sister in need but has not pity on them,
> how can the love of God be in that person? Dear
> children, let us not love with words or speech but
> with actions and in truth.
>
> (1 John 3:17-18)

As the first Christians "sold property and possessions to give to anyone who had need" (Acts 2:44-45), caring was a staple in the instructions of Paul in starting and developing Christian churches:

> Share with the Lord's people who are in need.
> (Romans 12:13)

> Therefore, as we have opportunity, let us do good
> to all people, especially to those who belong to the
> family of believers.
>
> (Galatians 6:10)

Paul connected our care for others to the will of Jesus Christ:

> Carry each other's burdens, and in this way you
> will fulfill the Law of Christ. (Galatians 6:2)

We need to remind ourselves that our work of caring does not merit or earn God's love. God freely gives us his love by pouring his love into our hearts through his Spirit.

God shows us his love for us in the work of Christ on the cross (Romans 5:8). There is nothing we can do to gain favor with God.

Thankfully, and necessarily, we are saved out of love alone--by grace through faith, not by our works (Ephesians 2:8-9).

Listening, praying, and caring is the way we pour out love for God and others. It is our love-filled response to the Gospel of God's love in Christ. Our works do not prepare us for God. Instead they are prepared by God for us to do:

> We are God's handiwork, created in Christ Jesus
> to do good works, which God prepared in advance
> for us to do. (Ephesians 2:10)

CARING EXAMPLES

Care is love in action, and God is the first to love and give. Jesus mentioned many ways God loves in the Beatitudes in Matthew 5:2-12.

As a blessing, God lovingly gives:

- The kingdom of heaven to the poor.
- Comfort to the mourning.
- The inheritance of the whole earth to the humble.
- Satisfaction to the hungry and thirsty.
- Mercy to the merciful.
- The future of seeing God to the pure of heart.

87

- The name "child of God" to the peacemakers.

- The kingdom of heaven to those who are persecuted for doing right.

- Rewards in heaven to the insulted, persecuted and slandered.

The power of God's love in us is evidenced in our generous and sacrificial giving. John the Baptist identified love in action in Luke 3:10-14:

- If anyone has two shirts, share one with the one who has none.

- If anyone has food, share with the one who has none.

- Give a fair tax rate as you collect taxes.

- Give others the freedom to do business without extorting them.

- Give people the benefit of the doubt.

- Give employers the opportunity to pay you what you deserve, without demanding more.

Going one step further, our giving in love relates to Judgment Day as Jesus described in the parable of the Sheep and the Goats in Matthew 25:31-46. Below is a list of the six caring actions toward Jesus identified as evidence toward a good verdict on the Day of Judgment:

- You gave me food when I was hungry.

- You gave me drink when I was thirsty.

- You gave me clothes when I was without.

- You gave me shelter when I had none.

- You gave me care when I was sick.

- You gave me a visit when I was in prison.

In the end, these simple, basic examples of *Care* are what identify us as Jesus' disciples. *Care* is sacrificial giving to help meet the smallest to the greatest needs of our neighbor in the name of Christ. When needs are before us, Jesus expects and commands that we open the floodgates of love, acting in loving ways.

Jesus made it personal, saying our obedience to God through our love for one another honors him:

> Jesus said, 'Truly I tell you, whatever you did for one of the least of these my brothers and sisters of mine, you did for me.' (Matthew 25:40)

FOLLOW-UP WITH CARE

As a practical matter, *Care* during gatherings with fixed time frames may need to be delayed, due to the specific need. In order for people to follow up, some contact information may be required.

If we seriously consider that we will be making hundreds, if not thousands, of contacts over a lifetime of LPC, finding a consistent and easy way for every Christian to exchange contact information is a big step in continuing care.

While we may be hesitant at first, we need to be proactive about intentionally sharing basic contact information to facilitate follow-up. Once love pours out of us, the flow doesn't stop just because group time is up. It is part of what Jesus described as going the extra mile (Matthew 5:41).

I've found the most effective tool is a prepared business card, which I simply call a *Care* Card. Yes, you can try to memorize the information, but we know how that goes for most people. Yes, you can scribble a name and number on someone's hand or a scrap of paper, but not everyone can read your handwriting. Yes, you can transfer contact information phone to phone, but not everyone has a smart phone or knows how to use it. Besides, you can always use those options as backup. A *Care* Card is still the most useful method of exchanging contact information.

Take a little time to consider the information you may want to share with others. A *Care* Card is easy to set up, easy to monitor by parents who create cards for their children, and it shows that you are serious about extending *Care* beyond the LPC group time to those who need it.

Here is a sample:

Once again, although there are other methods of obtaining contact information, such as name tags, directories, guest books, or registration tables, these are not as universally effective as *Care* Cards. The contact information needs to go with us when we leave our groups.

Think about meeting with a vegetable grower you meet at your local market. Even though you might remember their name and be able to search for their website, it is still more effective to take one of their business cards.

LPC is a business of the spiritual kind. It is the business we were created for. We want to become skilled and proficient at what we do. A business card can be a big help.

Care **Tips**

- **Keep in mind *Care* is love in action**—it matters what you do.

- **Acknowledge salvation in Christ**—our care is a reflection of Christ's love.

- **Nurture others through *Care***—we offer TLC (tender, loving care).

- **Live out your purpose**—care with all our heart, soul, mind and strength.

- **Be like God**—be generous.

- **Follow Jesus' example**—sacrifice.

- **Praise God**—in what you do and give.

- **Share**—with those in need.

- **Encourage others**—in love and good deeds.

- **Use *Care* Cards**—make follow-up easier.

- **Carry blank *Care* Cards**—you can ask for contact information from others.

8
LPC GROUPS
SMALLER IS BETTER

Time is critical. In order to effectively and efficiently love others through *Listen Pray Care*, we need time. We need to keep the number of people we care for in line with our natural time constraints. In the end, this means we need to keep groups small. I suggest—very small.

The goal of LPC groups is to love one another by specifically and deliberately, making sure:

- Each person is listened to, prayed and cared for.

- Each person listens to, prays, and cares for others. (Note: we invite but do not force people to pray.)

In LPC groups, we create small groups within larger groups, providing time for everyone to fully participate in LPC.

LPC GROUPS VS. SMALL GROUP MINISTRY

You may have already experienced the dynamics and intimacy that come with meeting in small groups. There are significant differences between typical church small groups and LPC groups:

- LPC groups are truly small. They are groups of two or three people.

- LPC groups are not stand-alone groups. They are formed *within* larger groups which have a broader or different purpose, such as Bible study, fellowship, education, small group ministry, service, athletics, worship or discipleship.

- LPC groups don't have members. Participation is fluid.

- LPC groups are self-led. Listening, praying, and caring are simple and easy to understand and accomplish. This eliminates the necessity for trained facilitators or leaders for each group.

- LPC groups are narrowly focused: they are formed with the express purpose of loving one another by practicing LPC.

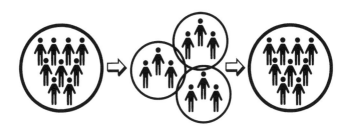

LARGE-TO-SMALL-TO-LARGE

Forming smaller groups within larger groups is a necessity. Picture the average family reunion. Family reunions are highly relational. After all, the people attending are related. Small groups naturally form within the larger gathering. It is the means by which we relate more personally with people at the gathering. Even if we wanted to, there is not enough time to relate to everyone in a large gathering.

Contrast this with a large group of people who are audience to a performance on a stage. This setting is the least intimate and relational. I am suggesting that an intentional and specific small group component be added to all your larger group gatherings, increasing the opportunity for everyone to participate and benefit from loving one another through LPC.

Youth groups are challenging communities. They provide a helpful example of intentionally forming small groups within larger groups. Games and relational ministry require the larger group to be regularly divided into smaller groups. Youth leaders learn how to divide a large group into smaller groups and put it back together again.

It is amazing to watch. With simple, basic directions, youth leaders can divide a group of 150 squirrely middle-schoolers into small groups, along with their visiting friends, in less than a minute. It takes even less time to re-assemble the large group. Simple tools and basic rules help things run smoothly.

Classroom teachers are also experts at creating smaller groups for interactive projects and discussion. It is part of the modular classroom concept.

Special seating arrangements and even modern chair designs, such as swivel chairs or desks on wheels, make it even easier to quickly form smaller groups on a regular basis.

In any setting, creating LPC groups will be under the direction of the large group leader. The leader will need to oversee breaking the large group into small groups of two or three and then back again.

Remember, most people don't overthink directions. They simply follow the leader they trust. Leaders that show confidence and are well prepared can help their group through most changes.

THE TIME FACTOR

Limited time is the most compelling reason to form small LPC groups within larger gatherings. If *each* person in a group engages in listening, praying, and caring, it takes a certain amount of time. For a picture of how this works in real time, we tried implementing LPC in a men's Bible study near my home.

Here is what we found. Early each Tuesday morning a group of 20+ men gather for a year-round Bible study. Over the years we have made an effort each week to *Listen Pray Care* with the men around the table as one large group. Our observations:

- On any given Tuesday, each man around the table has the opportunity to share something they are thankful for and/or needs to entrust to God, but only some in the group do this.

- If *half* of our group shares something personal, time for Bible study becomes scarce within our fixed time-frame.

- Those who do share can tend to be the same from week to week.

Our listening, praying and caring is incomplete if people are left out. We were not reaching the goal of everyone loving one another.

When we first tried forming LPC groups, we found that the groups started falling into natural time patterns.

As an experiment, we left the LPC group time open-ended to see how long it might take. The person to the left of the person sharing was designated to say the prayer.

This is what we discovered:

- The average person shared for four minutes.

- The average person prayed for three minutes.

- The average group of two took 14 minutes.

- The average group of three took 19 minutes.

- The average group of four (yes, we tried larger groupings) took 28 minutes.

The results above suggest that an average group of two or three needs a minimum of 15-20 minutes. Groups of four took too long for our time frame.

With careful planning, simple instruction, and regular practice, LPC groups can be taught to *Listen* and *Pray* with time efficiency.

We suggest the following *minimum* times for LPC groups:

- With practice, good leadership, and time consciousness: three people need a minimum of 10 minutes.

- At a more natural pace, three people need 15 minutes.

- Four people need 15 minutes minimum and 20 minutes at a more natural pace.

If you have serious time constraints, keep your groups small as we suggest. In the case where an LPC group finishes early, you can suggest that they pray together, pray silently or invite one person to share a little more.

Large group leaders may need to intentionally remind people to keep things simple and brief. Here are a few good phrases to repeat:

- God already knows what we need before we ask Him.

- Keep it simple.

- Children of God pray simply, like children of God. (You are a child of God, pray like a child of God.)

GETTING STARTED

First impressions are important. Design your first experience with LPC to end with a positive experience. A response of: "That sure was easy," and, "The time went quickly," is better than: "That took way too long."

In youth ministry we were trained to consider the positive feelings generated by having to set up more chairs for a meeting versus having a few people in a room full of empty chairs.

People requesting more time for LPC is better than allotting too much time, which forces people to either sit for long periods of inactivity or gives verbally gifted individuals too much freedom to dominate the group.

Of course, it's all up to you as the leader. You know your people better than anyone. Your goal is to make the whole LPC experience a comfortable and effective part of your gathering, using simple tools and simple rules.

Here is a sample of a 20 minute timetable for LPC:

- Introduction & Formation of LPC Groups (3 min.)

- LPC (15 min.)

- Closing Prayer & Reassembly (2 min.)

Here is a sample of a 12 minute time-table for LPC using a minimum timeframe:

- Introduction & Formation of LPC Groups (1 min.)

- LPC (10 min.)

- Closing Prayer & Reassembly (1 min.)

Here is a sample Q&A format for introducing LPC:

- **What are we doing?** *We are dividing into groups of two or three, following Jesus' command to love one another.*

- **How do we do this?** *Each person listens, prays, and cares. One person starts by sharing what they are thankful for or entrusting to God, then the person to the left prays for that person. Then move to the left.*

- **How long will this take?** *About 15 minutes. I will signal you when it is time to close.*

Note that there is no specific instruction for *Care*. *Care* will happen naturally as people are moved to express love to others in need. The possible ways to *Care* are infinite. It is your job as leader to encourage and support it.

Here is a sample introduction and closing for pastors and church leaders:

> L: We are committed to love one another as Christ has commanded his Church. In order to have an opportunity to love one another, we now form *Listen Pray Care* groups of two or three people.
>
> (When groups are formed the leader continues)
>
> L: Choose a person in your group to share something they are thankful for or something they need to entrust to God. When they finish, the person to the left will pray and also will be the next to share. If for some reason you are unable to pray, simply say, "Pass", indicating someone else in the group should offer a prayer. I will inform you when it is time to close.
>
> (When the time comes to close, the leader says)
>
> L: This concludes our *Listen Pray Care* time. Please pray with me.

Gracious Heavenly Father, we thank you for the amazing love you have shown us through your Son, Jesus Christ. Grant that the love we have shown one another, may reflect your love to those around us, that the world may see your love and turn to you in trust and hope. We thank you for hearing our prayers. We pray this in Jesus' name. Amen.

The assembly leader needs to gently move things along. Interpretations of the right ending time will be as numerous as the people in the room. This dynamic resembles the end of a college exam. Inevitably, there will be some who don't finish.

For our purposes, we do our best with the time we have set aside. Some listening, praying and caring is a good start. With practice, you will get better at reaching the goal within your scheduled time.

But what if...? Sometimes when someone begins to share a complicated life situation, it is like starting an avalanche. A certain individual may be hard-pressed to keep things short and simple. Some complicated relational problems require more than a few words of explanation.

In cases where more time is necessary, encourage people to arrange for a follow-up meeting or phone call. Certain issues need more time. Certain problems need better explanations.

Large group leaders may say:

> L: If you feel there is not enough time, we
> encourage you to arrange for a follow-up meeting
> or phone call.

If LPC groups get off-track with small-talk, story-telling, counseling, advising, arguing, etc. it is best to direct them back to the three basic activities of LPC.

Think again about a person whose clothes are on fire. There are many considerations and factors that could affect our method of handling flames on our clothing, but getting distracted or overcomplicated could mean disaster.

The basics are what we need to remember and do. Even a child can understand and remember how to *Listen Pray Care*. If groups stay focused on these three activities, they will stay on track.

ESSENTIAL LEADERSHIP

Even though LPC groups do not have leaders in each group, it is essential to have strong leadership overall to help get things started and to keep things on track. In training large group leaders to prepare people for LPC, we need to teach the practice of *gradually* releasing responsibility. Each person in every group needs to learn what to do and how to self-regulate their participation.

In the beginning this means that the leader takes time to show and explain to everyone how LPC is done, with the goal that they will learn to be responsible to do it on their own.

When they first try it, the large group leader might regularly observe and comment. Leaders may explain in real time what is expected to happen—essentially participating alongside them. Over time, the large group leader will discover less guidance is needed to get the desired result.

Make sure you give this process enough time. This could take months in some settings.

Remember, dumping responsibility to your LPC groups is different than gradually releasing it. It is like trying to get a group to paint a room for the first time by simply announcing, "Paint the room." Releasing responsibility too soon leads to ineffectiveness and inefficiency.

Just like a coach for an athletic team, leaders need to drill the fundamentals and work on skills training to create great players. It takes significant time. Be patient. The results will be worth it.

These are the components of strong LPC leadership:

- **Clear Vision**—you know what you want to accomplish.

- **Clear Plan**—you know how you are going to accomplish your goals.

- **Clear Communication**—you know what you need to say and how to say it.

- **Adequate Preparation**—for resistance to change, humble response to naysayers, and helping people understand and commit to a method that works (yes, it is not divine, but very effective).

- **Clear Evaluation of Success**—everyone listens, prays and cares. Everyone is listened to, prayed for, and cared for.

PERMISSION STATEMENTS

In order to give people freedom within LPC groups, large group leaders may decide to use some permission statements when establishing the ground rules for LPC groups such as:

- If you are not ready to pray, you have permission to pass when your turn comes.

- Children are welcome to participate as they are able.

- You have permission to limit your sharing and praying. God understands what you are going to say before you say it.

- You have permission to extend your care beyond our LPC group time through follow-up contact with each other.

- Feel free to exchange contact information.

FIVE-MINUTE WARNING

Five minutes before the end of your LPC group time, a chime or music can be used to signal it is time to wrap up the LPC activity. Quiet, live or recorded music may be gently played in the background. Countdown screens can be used, or any other method of informing everyone that you are nearing the end.

You may wish to include more detailed instructions about the five-minute warning at the beginning of your LPC group time. For instance, you might say:

> L: Music will begin to play five minutes before the end of our Listen Pray Care time. We encourage you to respectfully allow the opportunity for everyone in your group to share.

At the end of the LPC group time, the large group leader may offer a prayer for prayers unspoken and caring yet to take place in ongoing love for one another.

Here is a sample prayer:

> L: Heavenly Father, we thank you for the privilege of reflecting your love in Christ through our love for one another. In your mercy, remind us that the prayers left unspoken this day are known by you. We also pray for the care that is yet to take place in the days to come, that we would continuously show your love to those around us. We pray this in Jesus' name, Amen.

9
LPC CHALLENGES
PEOPLE DYNAMICS

There are certain challenges that are bound to present themselves when you engage people in *Listen Pray Care* groups. There is great variety in most groups. Different ages, different beliefs, different cultures, different viewpoints, different backgrounds, experiences, and problems. All of this adds up to the potential for challenges in our conversations with others.

I invite you to familiarize yourself with the common challenges below and the tips to cope with them.

FIRST TIMERS

Making guests and visitors feel comfortable in LPC groups is a challenge. In some churches, first timers may expect to observe and stay anonymous. LPC groups change that expectation.

I was pastor of a rural congregation in South Dakota where it was a tradition to ask any guests or visitors to stand up in the church and announce who they were. For family it was awkward, but marginally understandable. However, for total strangers visiting the church, it caused significant anxiety. Some reacted very negatively to the experience and some never returned.

On a positive note, the visitor of a church who finds themselves in an LPC group can be made to feel welcome and more comfortable. LPC groups are much less socially intimidating due to the small size of the group. Leaders give them permission to pass if they don't feel ready to pray.

I have found that if the LPC group time is introduced with clear instructions and guests stay with their hosts, most guests and visitors are just fine. The surroundings and people are new to them, so LPC groups are just a part of the new experience.

Tips

- **Give permission to pass**—this is a great way of helping visitors who are not ready to pray.

- **Avoid embarrassing guests**—pointing people out, criticizing their behavior, and forcing their participation should be avoided.

- **Allow guests to stay with their hosts**—don't split them apart into other LPC groups.

- **Teach members to explain LPC groups to their guests**—begin with, "we take loving one another seriously."

SHY

Talking in front of people can be intimidating. Praying can be downright terrifying. LPC groups can be challenging for people who are afraid of praying in front of others. The first step in facing this challenge is already in place. We have reduced the number of people in a group to the least intimidating size. Two or three people is far less intimidating than six or 20.

The second step involves time and repetition. It takes time to try something new and develop comfort with it. Hearing others pray is a good start. It helps bolster confidence.

My children wonder how their dad can stand up in front of hundreds of people and speak comfortably. In their heads they say, "I could never do that." As is the case with all anxiety that comes from trying new things, we survive with practice. Over time our fears diminish. I tell them, "Try speaking in front of people a hundred times, then come and tell me that you can't do it."

The most socially challenged age group is young adolescents. Every young person develops at a different pace physically, emotionally, intellectually, spiritually, and socially. A young person who is developed socially, but physically looks like a young child, feels awkward. That makes a group of adolescents a major challenge.

With their natural insecurities, we might assume adolescents would be the last group to tolerate the anxiety of speaking or praying in front of other teens or adults.

Yet, as a youth leader, I found they adapt much quicker than you might expect when given clear directions and peer support. I believe it is a myth that young people are not able to overcome the fear of speaking or praying in small groups. In my youth ministry experience, with few exceptions, they *all* participate.

As for mature adults, they have an even better chance of being comfortable with participation at the outset.

Paul told us of his confidence when facing challenges:

> I can do all this through [Christ] who gives me strength. (Philippians 4:13)

Tips

- **Be patient**—shy people tend to take their time warming up to others. Give them lots of room for adjustment.

- **Invite participation**—never force it.

- **Provide focus**—"All we ask is that you listen to others in your group and share something simple."

- **Trust the leader**—comfort in LPC groups has more to do with trusting the gathering leader, than overcoming insecurities.

DIFFERENT SKILL LEVELS

There can be a wide range of skill levels present in LPC group participants. Young and old, introverted and extroverted, shy and confident, all can be together in the same setting. Just as a beach swimming area can accommodate everything from non-swimmers to Olympic swimmers, LPC groups are small and flexible enough to accommodate any skill level.

God is concerned about your heart, not your skill level. Listening and praying should be simple. You can bring your normal skill levels and do just fine. Anyone can do this. Also, everyone can get better with practice. In LPC groups, all we need is open ears to *Listen*, open hearts to *Pray*, and open arms to *Care*.

Tips

- **Encourage children**—it helps them in groups with adults.

- **Explain simple prayer**—a child's prayer is the standard, even for adults, not the other way around. The heart is what matters, not the words.

- **Be patient**—everyone gets better with practice.

CONFIDENTIALITY AND THE THREE HURTS

Things heard and said in LPC groups need to stay there. Confidentiality is important. What we learn about others is not to be used in an *unloving* way. This means keeping things confidential and not using what someone shares for gossip, betrayal or slander.

Confidentiality, though, is not absolute. There are three kinds of hurt that need to be reported if revealed in LPC groups: hurting self, hurting others, or being hurt.

Revealing a deep problem with one of the three hurts in a small group setting can be a cry for help.

If someone reveals one of the three hurts, take it seriously. Ask for advice from a trusted leader after the group time. It might be helpful to develop guidelines for getting help for someone who reveals they are suffering from one of the three hurts.

Tips

- **Be honest about limited confidentiality**—"We keep what is shared in LPC groups confidential unless there is a safety issue. In love, we cannot promise total confidentiality."

- **Provide accessible help**—create easy access to responsible leaders for those with safety concerns.

FIXERS AND SAVIORS

Fixers and Saviors find it difficult to listen, especially listening to understand. In their minds, the listening we do in LPC groups is for fixing problems and saving the lost and erring. This can sidetrack effective listening. Instead of fully hearing and understanding others, Fixers and Saviors are preoccupied with providing remedies, solutions, behavioral advice, and rescues.

Instead of receiving healthy feedback such as, "I hear you and understand," people in the group get, "Here is what you should do."

This is a common failure in human communication, and this is one challenge that should be periodically highlighted by assembly leaders while introducing LPC group time. Regular reminders can be very helpful and make people feel more comfortable.

Tips

- **Be clear**—fixing and saving are not our goals.

- **Review the LPC group goals**—in love, everyone is listened to, prayer for, and cared for and everyone listens, prays and cares.

- **Encourage one another**—build each other up in love.

- **Practice humility**—consider others better than yourself. Trust God with the rest.

BLACK HOLES

Staying on subject is not everyone's strong point. You may find some people are inclined to jump from subject to subject and have difficulty completing a point or thought. They can suck the life out of a small group. Usually, with a little help from others in the group, people can be encouraged to stay the course and keep it focused, short and sweet.

If, as a leader, you have to address a person directly about this, discuss it with them outside of your LPC group time. When facing distractions in your group, act in genuine love, just like you would with family.

Encourage each person to stay focused and explain how helpful it is. Remember, the key is to show love—lots of love.

Tips

- **Bear with one another in love**—some people are naturally distracted and struggle with staying on track.

- **Don't embarrass others**—speaking to a person after group time or getting assistance from a trusted leader is good way to address a problem with the least amount of embarrassment.

- **Accommodate special needs**—find someone who can accompany a person with special needs during your LPC group time to provide guidance and encouragement.

Section 3

LPC Leadership

10
CHURCH LEADERS
SERVING GOD

Pastors-Elders-Deacons-Evangelists
Church Planters-Missionaries-Chaplains

As a leader in the Christian church, you have a high calling in this life. You have a front row seat to the challenges and victories in God's non-stop efforts to seek and save the lost.

It is rewarding to see someone turn from sin, death and the devil to the one true God through the sharing of the Gospel of Christ in your ministry. It is satisfying to reassure a saint of the hope of heavenly glory that awaits them as they close their eyes in death. It is invigorating to watch God's people bravely share the Good News with neighbors and loved ones as God's Spirit moves them.

Your work may involve leading a church, planting new churches, reaching out to new people groups, or doing the humble work of holding up the hands of your local church staff as they lead the disciples of Christ. Your leadership is crucial to the future of Christianity, and its world impact.

I was drawn to church leadership by the wonderful example of my father, a great church leader. His passion for proclaiming the Gospel in gentle tones was closely matched by his deep compassion for people, just like Christ. I watched as he modeled deep love for God and others in all his work.

The leaps of faith he took during his ministry in the inner city of Milwaukee were stunning and inspiring. In retirement, one of his few laments was wishing he had the chance to implement the practice of LPC in the churches he served.

While you may direct the first steps of transition to LPC in your church's ministry to existing smaller groups in your church, the time will come when you will need to consider practicing LPC in weekend worship gatherings.

If you are starting a new church, it is the perfect time to consider integrating LPC in your weekend services, before local traditions are formed.

My calling as a church leader included the privilege of planting and serving in new churches. I understand the strong drive to move forward, the endless hours, the heartbreaking failures and the witness of God's pure grace and blessing.

I also have served churches on the other end of the spectrum that have few members remaining—mostly elderly with few programs, who wonder how long their beloved church will last. No matter what kind of church you serve, I believe each and every church can benefit from learning and practicing LPC as a way to strengthen relationships.

Listen Pray Care is a relational strategy for loving one another in your church gatherings—including Sunday mornings.

LPC benefits include:

- Your people advance beyond words and speech to actions and truth (1 John 3:18). They practice what you preach under your leadership.

- The visible mark of the church becomes clearly visible—love for one another (John 13:35). This is important for members and visitors.

- Sundays can become ground zero for training in LPC, preparing people to practice LPC in every other Christian gathering.

With careful planning, prayer, and Spirit-led leadership, people stay on course and celebrate loving one another as a special church family every time you gather.

HISTORY AND THEOLOGY

Sound doctrine and practice are very important. Review the Scripture passages in this book. Deeply explore the command of Christ to love one another. This will help you when you need to explain the purpose of LPC.

Historically, the church has been protective of what we do in our gatherings. The intention was, and is, to prevent false doctrine or damaging practices from creeping in. That protective attitude makes sense.

We don't want to allow change to hurt or damage the Body of Christ. It can lead to disaster.

However, even rigid liturgical churches have freedom and flexibility built into their gatherings. This allows good, safe, and spiritually healthy change necessary to the Church, to be brought by God through the Spirit to our benefit. If you look in the Church's past, a wide variety of liturgies, hymnals, service books, prayers, Bible translations, languages, rituals and practices have changed even within the most conservative churches.

My father's church used a liturgy *in German* every Sunday, opposite our English service. You can imagine the difficult transition for the congregation when they decided to change the language of their worship services to English. Local churches have always exercised the freedom to change practices or add ceremonies.

By regularly integrating LPC groups into your church setting, you will be creating a new church family tradition. It's a good, sound decision to love one another by practicing LPC.

The theology is sound. The basics are sure:

- Jesus declared that love for one another is the defining mark of the disciples of Christ (John 13:35).

- Our heavenly Father loved us by sending Jesus to display his love on the cross for us to see, hear, and believe (John 3:16-17).

- As new creations, we are to love as Christ loved us (John 13:34).

This is our work—to equip God's people for their life of love according to God's command and provision poured out through his Spirit. We can take steps toward that dream by practicing LPC. This is what Christ has gifted us for:

> So, Christ himself gave...the pastors and teachers, to equip his people for works of service, so that the body of Christ may be built up. (Ephesians 4:11-12)

> From him the whole body, joined and held together by every supporting ligament, grows and builds itself up in love, as each part does its work. (Ephesians 4:16)

A NEW SOLA

The teaching of love for one another is as critical as the teaching of salvation by grace through faith. After studying this subject for years, I suggest we might need to create a new *Sola* for our day—*Sola Amor* (love alone).

During my seminary training, one of my mentors looked through my sermon assignment and said, "This needs to be changed. You are spending time teaching *things*, rather than preaching salvation by God's grace in Christ. You need to keep the main thing, the main thing."

If God's love for, in and through us qualifies as a main thing Christ taught, we need to make it a priority too. We get too easily distracted.

During the Reformation, Church reformers kept faith vs. works in the forefront of theological discussion. It was a helpful way to steer the church in a Scriptural direction, given the prevalent teaching of *salvation by works*.

Today, keeping love in the theological forefront is imperative. The fact that some reduce love in their teaching to a feeling or a fruit, should not deter us.

It is time to boldly move beyond the *milk* of teaching salvation by faith vs. works to the *meat* of teaching how love, sourced in the heart of God himself, is expressed by faith in love toward God and one another. Paul described it as "the most excellent way" (1 Corinthians 12:31b).

In some ways the subject of love resembles faith in that we can falsely teach that man's faith/love is a work vs. gift meriting the favor of God. True faith and true love come from God, not from us. He works faith in our hearts and pours his love into us and through us. There is Spirit-wrought faith and Spirit-wrought love.

God is the source. We are the vessels and the instruments.

Our current struggle to maintain our theological anchors reflects similar struggles during the time of the Reformation. In the 1500's, the question about the contribution of merit, worthiness or righteous works toward our salvation was at the center of Christian dialog.

Bible passages were used to support the view that it was God's work alone.

This passage was, perhaps, used the most:

> For it is by grace you have been saved, through faith—and this is not from yourselves, it is the gift of God—not by works, so that no one can boast. (Ephesians 2:8-9)

Special summary phrases began to circulate among reformers. To say, "God's grace is all that is needed, not works" the Latin phrase *Sola Gratia*—grace alone, was used. To say, "Faith is all that is needed, not works" the phrase *Sola Fide*—faith alone, was used. To say, "Christ's work on the cross is all that is needed, not works" the phrase *Sola Christus*—Christ alone, was used. Two others also made their rounds: *Sola Scriptura*—Scripture alone, and *Soli Deo Gloria*—to God alone be the glory.

Paul taught that *love* is the greatest when comparing faith, hope and love (1 Corinthians 13:13). Paul might have said something like this: if you have *Scripture* to teach the norms of faith and life, *grace* to describe the unmerited work of God, *faith* to receive the gospel, *Christ* to complete the work of God and *glory* given to God, but have not love, you gain nothing.

Put another way: God's love alone is the source and motive for his grace alone, through faith alone, in Christ alone, as Scripture alone attests to the glory of God alone.

According to Paul, *Sola Amor*—love alone, is the greatest. It is the most excellent.

Today, the world Church needs to get deeper and focus on the teaching and practice of God's love in Christ toward others. Next to God himself, love is the most universal Biblical subject.

Love is behind our existence, identity and salvation. Everything we study and experience in this life is founded in God's message of *Sola Amor*.

This is perfectly expressed in Psalms:

> "I will sing of the LORD's great love forever."
> (Psalm 89:1a)

LOVE TIES TO SACRIFICIAL WORSHIP

God is glorified when his love flows through us to others; he is worshiped. In Christian circles we talk about the worship of God as a central Christian activity. The Scriptures teach that the flow of love from the heart of God, to us and to others, is part of our worship of God. Therefore, we worship God when we offer ourselves to his work of love through *Listen Pray Care*.

Paul said:

> I urge you, brothers and sisters, in view of God's mercy, to offer your bodies as a living sacrifice, holy and pleasing to God—this is your true and proper worship. (Romans 12:1)

Living our lives like Jesus, who sacrificed himself for us, is central to our worship. We know this and teach this. Most local church worship services include prayers for each other and offerings to support the local church, feed the poor, and help the homeless. God is glorified when we love our neighbors. I believe we can do this in a better way by integrating LPC groups into our worship settings.

Old Testament sacrifices in temple worship created strong imagery. Peter wrote about a new Christian priesthood offering sacrifices:

> You also, like living stones, are being built into a
> spiritual house to be a holy priesthood, offering
> spiritual sacrifices acceptable to God through
> Jesus Christ. (1 Peter 2:5)

Jesus tied our love for one another to our offerings at the altar of God:

> If you are offering your gift at the altar and there
> remember that your brother or sister has
> something against you, leave your gift there in
> front of the altar. First go and be reconciled to
> them; then come and offer your gift.
> (Matthew 5:23-24)

The writer of the book of Hebrews was extensively knowledgeable about temple worship and wrote about the future of worship and sacrificial love for others that came through Christ:

> Through Jesus, therefore, let us continually offer
> to God a sacrifice of praise—the fruit of lips that
> openly profess his name. And do not forget to do
> good and to share with others, for with such
> sacrifices God is pleased.
> (Hebrews 13:16)

One of my favorite Bible verses directs us to offer and sacrifice to God just as Jesus did:

Be kind and compassionate to one
another, forgiving each other, just as in Christ
God forgave you.
Follow God's example, therefore, as dearly loved
children and walk in the way of love, just as Christ
loved us and gave himself up for us as a fragrant
offering and sacrifice to God. (Ephesians 4:32–
5:2, emphasis mine)

By our sacrificial love for one another, God our Father receives our worship and is glorified:

This is to my Father's glory, that you bear much
fruit, showing yourselves to be my disciples.
(John 15:8)

Sunday gatherings...worship of God...love one another...OK, connect the dots!

CHRISTIAN GATHERINGS

The Bible's first descriptions of Christian church gatherings included intentional and deliberate expressions of sacrificial love for one another.

Luke's record is vivid:

They devoted themselves to the apostles'
teaching and to fellowship, to the breaking of
bread and to prayer...All the believers were
together and had everything in common. They
sold property and possessions to give to anyone
who had need. (Acts 2:42–45)

As a child, I was taught the passage below to underscore the requirement for regular attendance in my local church. As I look at the passage again, it amazes me that this passage does not speak of worship of God in the traditional sense. Instead, the entire verse is directed to our love for one another:

> Let us consider how we may *spur one another on toward love and good deeds*, not giving up meeting together, as some are in the habit of doing, but *encouraging one another*—and all the more as you see the Day approaching. (Hebrews 10:24-25, emphasis mine)

Love for God and one another was a central part of the gatherings of early Christians, in keeping with the directives they had received—both new and old:

> Be very careful to love the LORD your God.
> (Joshua 23:11)
>
> Be devoted to one another in love.
> (Romans 12:10a)
>
> Dear children, let us not love with words or speech but with actions and in truth.
> (1 John 3:18)

The Biblical description of our life under God provides a powerful motive to re-examine what we actually do today when we gather in Jesus' name.

For four Bible stories of LPC in the life of Jesus, see the Appendix.

A MATTER OF TRAINING

When I first began researching the topic of loving one another, I had to look in the mirror and ask, "Am I the best person to teach about building relationships in Christ's Church? I'm not trained for this." Thinking back to my training as a pastor, I was trained to be an expert in theology and preaching, not relationships.

Wanting to love one another in our Christian gatherings is like dreaming of visiting exotic destinations but never planning for it. We will never arrive if we don't know a way to get there. Without a plan, we will forever dabble in the *milk* of worshipping God without the *meat* of loving one another.

If you look to the past to inform our future, the past centuries of Christianity have been in serious need for a way to intentionally, specifically, and deliberately love one another. Given our relationally sensitive culture, we are even more in need of a change.

The first step in resolving this issue is admitting it is a problem. Then we need a way to address the problem provided by LPC.

Tips

- **Check your theology**—you are responsible to make sure that what you are doing is aligned with the Bible and the practices of your church body.

- **Start with the basics**—pray and do your homework.

- **Plan for change**—include LPC in your short and long-range strategic planning.

- **Integrate LPC into your mission, purpose and values**—the clearer you can be, the more aligned you will be in your implementation. As I have said earlier, LPC is part of the mission of the church— the work of making disciples and being marked as disciples in word and deed.

- **Select your favorite Bible references**—your conversations on this topic will stay anchored if you are able to share a few Bible references by memory. My favorite verses include Hebrews 10:24-25, Ephesians 4:32-5:2, John 13:34-35, Ephesians 4:16, and 1 John 4:7-8.

- **Network**—with volunteers and professionals. Youth leaders and teachers are experienced with breaking larger groups into smaller ones. Seek their advice.

- **Capitalize on fresh starts**—if you are starting a new worship service or new church plant, it is a perfect time to integrate LPC.

- **Brush up on your change management**—get advice by reading and networking before you make a change as big as altering worship settings.

- **Practice what you preach**—it is critical that you practice LPC as a leader. Participate in an LPC group and experience how it works.

- **Start small**—consider starting with the existing small to medium-sized groups in your church before making the change in your largest group settings.

- **Evaluate regularly**—don't forget to evaluate your progress at regular intervals. Make changes to your approach as needed.

11
CHRISTIAN EDUCATORS
TEACHING TRUTH

College and Seminary Professors
Parochial School Teachers
Sunday School Teachers
Bible Study Leaders-Small Group Leaders

The Church is blessed by its teachers. If you are a professional or volunteer teacher in a Christian setting, you have a treasured calling to follow in the footsteps of our Lord Jesus who was called *Rabboni*—which means *teacher* (John 20:16).

Teachers shape hearts and minds. That's what Jesus Christ was all about. In his footsteps, you train our upcoming generations. You have the opportunity, through the Spirit, to influence the lives of the young and old, by helping them grow and mature in the truth of God's Word and their faith and life in Christ.

To me, that is exciting!

When I was a religion instructor at a nearby Christian high school, I woke up each day excited. I was thankful that God had given me another day to help my students learn what it means to believe in and follow Christ. I loved the thrill of watching students learn and grow. I understand the drive and commitment you have to be a good teacher.

Many of you have sacrificed much to be an educator. Whether you are a volunteer, a professional, a substitute, or a facilitator in a small group, you pour yourself into the opportunity to help your students grow deeper in their relationship with God.

Some of you practice team-based activities in your classes, dividing your class into groups for projects, discussion, debate, etc. LPC requires you to divide your class into groups of two or three.

If you design or write curriculum, your skills can be very helpful in helping teach the basics of LPC. Having spent time writing, developing, and coordinating Sunday School curriculums and catechetic instruction, I know the value of having good materials from which to teach. Maybe you can assist your school or church by writing some curriculum suggestions for implementing LPC. You are a valuable asset!

Tips

- **Teach the purpose of LPC**—to share God's love in Christ through love for one another.

- **Pursue the goal of LPC**—everyone listened to, prayed for, and cared for as everyone listens, prays and cares.

- **Plan regular practice of LPC**—when you can, build this into your regular class routine.

- **Slowly release responsibility**—self-leadership may take some time to develop in LPC groups, especially in the young.

- **Stick to your scheduled time**—LPC should not interfere with your course work.

- **Discipline privately**—address serious concerns with individual behavior in private.

- **Be sensitive to non-believing students**—they should not be required to pray, but encouraged to do so when ready.

12
YOUTH LEADERS
BUILDING COMMUNITY

Professional Youth Workers
Youth Leaders-Youth Counselors
Youth Camp Leaders
Youth Mission & Servant Event Leaders

I remember one of my first experiences as a youth pastor. As I entered the youth room filled with the hustle and bustle of adolescents, I noticed some of the students pointing to a table near the corner of the room. A middle school student had climbed under the table and was hugging his knees with a look of apprehension on his face. This was his first youth group meeting. The only thing he could think of was to hide!

I ended up on my knees, crawling under the table to talk with the student. We talked quietly for a while in his safe place, while the rest of the room was oblivious. With a little friendly coaxing he finally came out of hiding. Together, we began the adventure of meeting new people.

I later realized, all it took was someone to care enough to enter his frightening world for a moment and listen to him. It was an eye-opening experience as a youth pastor!

As youth leaders and workers, I'm sure you have similar stories to tell. These stories inspire us. They bring tears to our eyes and warm our hearts. We have a passion to help young people discover what life is about and how God loves and cares for them throughout their days. Although some look at our disorganized desks and cars and say we lack organizational skills, our relational senses are first rate.

We want to make a difference in the lives of young people in their relationship with God and the people in the world around them.

Whether you are a professional youth worker or a volunteer youth leader in your community, you have the precious opportunity to mentor young people.

Some of the greatest influences in my life came from humble youth leaders at my local church. They believed in me and challenged me to develop a love and thirst for God. They used love and compassion to shape my view of how we are to treat one another. They showed me how to love, even in difficult circumstances. They inspired me to become a youth leader myself!

Youth leaders know the importance of community. We proudly label our work *relational youth ministry.* Relationships and community building are at the core of every youth ministry setting, including youth groups, camps, counseling, mentor programs, Bible studies, campus activities, gatherings, conferences, worship events, mission events, servant trips, and outreach programs.

LPC is a simple strategy for building community among youth in Christ. LPC groups encourage everyone to participate and contribute to the goal, giving each youth the opportunity to grow and experience real and tangible expressions of love.

Everyone listens, prays, and cares so that everyone is listened to, prayed for and cared for. This is the basic way we show love for one another.

Listen, alone, is a huge step in building community. Young people are notoriously distracted listeners. Give them guidance and practice, and you can transform their fickle listening into the powerful skill of listening to understand.

Pray and *Care* resulting from careful listening becomes more personal and impactful. Compare this to popcorn-style prayer that can be short, clipped, and non-inclusive.

Simple is better. You know that our children will struggle, as we have, with loving one another. It is good to have a simple, memorable, and understandable way to teach love for one another.

Create a vision for youth to learn LPC early on and encourage them to practice it throughout their lives.

As a youth leader, you will be responsible to introduce the practice of LPC in your group settings. The desired result is that our youth communities become relationally connected in love, like family.

Young people will take the skills they learn with them into adulthood and future family life. They may even walk in your footsteps and become leaders of the next generation.

Tips

- **Teach parents about LPC**—encourage them to try LPC at home during or after dinner.

- **Keep it simple**—stick to the basics in LPC.

- **Have a plan**—don't just drop this on your group and co-workers without preparing them.

- **Stay the course**—your constant leadership will be needed.

- **Use simple phrases**—*God's love is what we share when we Listen, Pray, and Care.*

- **Share the results**—if your youth group is the first official group to practice LPC in your church, share your progress and results with your church leadership. You just might influence a change in the whole church.

- **Keep track of time**--yes, you have to.

- **Keep LPC groups small**—fight the temptation to allow more than three people in LPC groups. Distinguish between LPC groups and traditional small groups. Most traditional small groups are large in comparison. If you have four in a group, it *might* work if you have ample time available (e.g. 30 minutes).

- **Network with your leaders**—your Children's Ministry, Sunday School and Vacation Bible School teachers may benefit from networking to help generate creative ways to incorporate LPC in their groups and classes.

13
WORSHIP LEADERS
GLORIFYING GOD

Worship Leaders-Worship Team Leaders
Music Directors-Ushers & Greeters
Choir Directors-Drama Directors-Tech Directors

Nothing compares to the experience of leading people in the worship of God. As people express their love for God in one voice, there is a heavenly sound to the symphony of God's people. It is a little glimpse of heaven. As I tell my daughters who play guitar, everything starts with a well-tuned instrument and the heart to play it. As we worship God, our hearts, voices, and instruments meld in praise of our God and King.

Ever since I was young, I have looked up to worship leaders—whether they are pastors, contemporary worship leaders, cantors or even Christian bands on tour.

After learning piano and guitar, I found myself leading worship in everything from summer camps, youth groups, chapels, church starts, conferences, and retreats. I have fond memories of starting a contemporary worship service, which we called Impact 909, in my church in Sioux Falls, South Dakota. I still grab my keyboard and play in a men's worship band for an annual state men's retreat and periodically lead worship on weekends for a local community church.

If this is your calling, you are blessed with a beautiful opportunity to serve in the church of Christ. Whether you lead a choir, a band, a drama team or an entire worship service, you not only lead music and worship, you lead people. This can be rewarding and difficult.

Working with artists and musicians can be a delicate task. (I think it has something to do with our extensive use of our right brains. In my experience, musicians can be a bit eccentric.) With love and patience your worship teams and groups can become like family.

In order to prepare for practicing LPC, start by becoming familiar with the theology behind LPC by reading the Scriptural background provided in this book.

Putting LPC into practice will affect two areas of your work. The first is your rehearsals. Identify your role in rehearsals. Ask yourself if you are only rehearsing music for a performance or also helping build up the body of Christ.

If you already have a prayer or devotion as part of your rehearsal, you have already decided the latter. Now you need to consider how to implement LPC in your rehearsals.

The second place LPC affects your work is in the worship setting. If your church includes LPC in your worship setting, you can lead by example and help facilitate the LPC group time.

In a sense, we already love one another when we pray in the general prayers, although a key component is missing—we are not listening to each other. The practice of LPC deepens our prayer and care for each other by intentionally listening to each person's needs and then praying and caring.

You may be familiar with the traditional idea that worship is limited to an exclusive focus on God. The idea is that we don't focus on people. There is supposed to be an audience of One.

In reality, it is both.

All churches show love for one another to some degree in our greetings, offerings for the poor, and prayers. God is to be the sole recipient of our worship, but our *acts of worship* include intentionally loving one another.

This is the most important concept for you to understand and teach as a worship leader who is keeping the big picture in view.

You will find the important connection between an act of love toward others and an act of worship clearly presented in this Bible passage:

> Follow God's example, therefore, as dearly loved children and walk in the way of love, just as Christ loved us and gave himself up for us *as a fragrant offering and sacrifice to God.*
> (Ephesians 5:1-2, emphasis mine)

What was the *way of love* commanded by Christ?

> A new command I give you: Love one another. As I have loved you, so you must love one another.
> (John 13:34)

Notice how our love for God includes love for others, just like Christ demonstrated. This love for others is our offering and sacrifice to God. Offerings and sacrifices are worship in the strongest Biblical terms. There should be a vertical *and* horizontal aspect to our worship of God.

From this basic understanding, we might ask a new question, "What is the best way to love others in Sunday worship?" This is new for many worship leaders, including myself when I first discovered this truth.

Love for one another is not very personal, direct, and deliberate in most of the worship services I encounter. Yet, according to Christ, we are all obligated to love our brothers and sisters. It is part of our worship of God.

It is part of our regular meeting together:

> And let us consider how we may spur one another
> on toward love and good deeds, not giving up
> meeting together, as some are in the habit of
> doing, but encouraging one another—and all the
> more as you see the Day approaching. (Hebrews
> 10:24-25)

As worship leaders, we not only have to spend time organizing and planning worship through Word and song, we must do our part to help organize and plan a time and method for God's people to love one another as Christ commanded. This is an essential part of our whole picture of worship.

This is where the practice of LPC shines. You will need to plan the time to form LPC groups, such as an expanded prayer time, and help with musical transitions as needed.

YOU AND YOUR PASTOR

You must cultivate a good relationship with your pastor. Like a good teacher in a classroom or a coach for a team, pastors are in charge and responsible for everything that happens in worship. They say things to express their feelings of ownership and responsibility like a teacher who says, "When I teach *my* class..." and a coach who says, "When *my* team goes out on the field..." Pastors will say "When people in *my* church help out..." or "*My* worship leader says..."

Please understand that what goes on in church is very *personal* to your pastor. I have worn the hats of pastor and worship leader many times. Pastors are very protective of the service, which you may have already observed. They may express displeasure if the songs take too much time or if a worship leader steals the thunder of the message.

That is because the worship service is, as I said, very *personal* to pastors. It is at the heart of their work and calling. Everything that is said and done reflects on them. They put a lot of time into the message for the service.

Pre-empting a pastor's message is akin to your pastor introducing a new song you wrote by singing your song before you come on stage to reveal it to the world.

Remember, worship leaders need to work closely with their pastors. Most of your work will be *with* pastors, but you are still *under* them. Show them the respect and love they deserve. They are your overseers. In Christ, they will respond with love and respect for you.

Tips

- **Learn about worship from Ephesians 5:1-2**— love for one another is a fragrant offering and sacrifice to God.

- **Try new ideas**—instead of inserting LPC into the general prayer time in the weekend service, integrate it as part of your worship set.

- **Consider the vertical and horizontal aspects of worship**—we are not turning away from God when we turn to each other to *Listen Pray Care*. Notice that the two great commandments do not use the word *worship*. Worship matters—but love matters more. Music matters, but love matters more. Our actions in love for God and others gives glory and honor to God. It is an integral part of our worship.

- **Make LPC part of your rehearsals**—our love for each other practiced in our rehearsals flows into our praise and worship of God in our church gatherings. It also shows that love matters more.

- **Practice LPC in all music groups**—instrumental groups, adult choirs, children's choirs, bands, ensembles, quartets, bell choirs, etc.

- **Carefully plan for and lead LPC group time**— with careful planning and directions you can complete LPC groups in 10-12 minutes.

- **Practice LPC in your tech, drama, usher, greeter and stage teams**—every worship support team can benefit from the practice of LPC with one another.

- **Consider music as a means not an end**—learn the significance of full, deep worship of God without any music. Silence can be powerful. Deep, meaningful worship also includes our listening, praying, and caring.

- **Respect your pastor**—pastors are called servants in charge of the worship service. You honor Christ by loving and serving them.

- **Take time to *Listen Pray Care* with your pastor**—it will deepen your relationship with your pastor.

14
HOME LEADERS
SHAPING LIVES

Parents-Guardians-Grandparents-Spouses
Friends-Relatives-Dating Couples
Caregivers-Mentors

Leadership at home is one of the most crucial roles in life. Raising children, working to support the home, and living a life of love for God and others is an ongoing, 24/7 endeavor. A supportive, loving home is the best incubator for faith development. With your leadership, home leaders steer the family in the right direction.

God places us in many different situations and contexts. In the case of the leader at home, you have the responsibility to provide 24/7 support for the faith development of everyone in the home. At the core of the home is love for God and one another.

One the of the best Bible passages on leadership at home is Moses' directive to the people of Israel:

> Love the LORD your God with all your heart and with all your soul and with all your strength. These commandments that I give you today are to be on your hearts. Impress them on your children. Talk about them when you sit at home and when you walk along the road, when you lie down and when you get up. Tie them as symbols on your hands and bind them on your foreheads. Write them on the doorframes of your houses and on your gates.
>
> (Deuteronomy 6:5-9)

Love for our God who loves and saves, starts at home. For some of you, since you are the first follower of Jesus Christ in your home, this is your mission field. Some start their journey of faith by receiving God's love through others before recognizing and acknowledging the source and reason.

As a leader in your home, you are a 24/7 witness to God's love flowing through you in love for God and others. If given a chance to explain, you tell your family about Christ's love on the cross. Christ shows us, in person, how deep the Father's love is for us and how he equips us to share that love in our relationships with God and others.

GOD'S LOVE IS WHAT WE SHARE

In general, what we learn at home is the basis for what we share outside the home. We know that teaching good manners is important not just for home life, but also life in and among the neighbors around us. We know that teaching respect for the law is important, first at home, and in our keeping of the law away from home.

The way we live in relationship with each other at home becomes the way we live with others outside the home.

What we learn at home stays with us for a lifetime. We repeat things we learn at home such as, "Wash your hands before you eat," and "Say please and thank you." In Wisconsin, I taught my growing children the basics of driving a car in changing weather: "In fog and snow, lights on low."

The Christian parenting goal is to teach our children how to answer the question, "How do we show love for one another?" Our goal is that our children easily and confidently answer, "We listen, pray, and care." As a leader in your home, you can teach the basics of loving one another by regularly practicing *Listen Pray Care* in your family. This way your children will develop the critical skills they need for a lifetime.

Here is an example of a home dialog.

> Chad burst into the kitchen after school. His mother was washing pots and pans in the sink.
>
> "Hi Chad," she said cheerfully, "how was your day?
>
> "Oh, fine Mom," he said, shrugging his shoulders. He set his backpack down and leaned against the wall.
>
> "How are things going with that girl you like?" she said, eyes sparkling.
>
> His shoulders slumped. "Oh, not so good...I'm not sure she thinks I care about her."
>
> "Oh really? Tell me more," she said, turning to look at him.
>
> "Well, she just seems to think I think only about myself—but that's not true. I think about her all the time. How did she get the idea I don't care about her?
>
> "Do you talk during the day?
>
> "Yeah, we sit together at lunch, but I seem to do all the talking. I really don't know..."
>
> "Maybe it's a matter of *how* you show you like her," she said.
>
> "What do you mean?"
>
> "Well, in our family we show that we care about

each other by listening to each other, and praying, right? Let's start with the first one: do you really listen to her? Are you interested in what she thinks and feels? Do you let her know that what she says is important to you when you are talking to her?" Her tone was soft and kind.

Chad thought for a moment. "Well, maybe," he said. "Listening might be the answer. It's just hard to do when she doesn't say much." He crossed his arms and sighed.

"Give it a try, Chad. It just might help," she offered.

BENDING THE CONVERSATION

A good friend and I meet periodically for lunch. He bends the conversation with our server into a practice of LPC. When the food arrives, he says, "We are about to pray over our meal. Is there anything you would like us to pray for?"

Initially, some servers are speechless, but on quite a few occasions, they will share what is on their heart. It makes our prayer before the meal quite meaningful. We show ongoing *Care* by following up on the prayer the next time we visit and see the server we prayed for. We also tangibly help if we can.

Try it the next time you are out for a meal.

Tips

- **Keep it simple**—the basics are just that, basic.

- **Tell stories**—share your own successes and challenges in loving others.

- **Make time for LPC**—make family time for *Listen Pray Care*. Meal time is a good start.

- **Make LPC part of your bedtime routine**—try listening, praying, and caring at the end of the day.

- **Practice LPC on vacation**—plan time for LPC when you are on vacation. If you miss your weekend church service because you are on the road, take some extended time for LPC as part of your Sunday "make-up".

- **Introduce friends to LPC**—teach your family that our casual and formal interactions with Christians such as meeting at a coffee shop, or going out on a date, includes listening, praying, and caring. It doesn't have to be formally started and ended, but you know when you are doing it.

- **Practice what you teach**—practice LPC during the course of your day. Your children will learn LPC is a basic of life.

- **Create a family phrase for LPC**—describe your basic understanding of how to love one another. I use *God's love is what we share when we Listen, Pray, and Care.*

- **Teach about LPC in your everyday conversation with your family members**—dive into the tough challenges. Focus on how to love people who don't believe in God and how to love friends, acquaintances, co-workers, bosses, police officers, sports team members, coaches, classmates, and roommates. Share how you love people you don't like.

- **Give permission to pass**—respect others. Prayer is *by permission only.* People who do not want to pray or to be prayed for, should have your respect. They are free to exempt themselves from your offer to pray. We don't force faith in God on others.

- **Resolve your conflicts**—when there is conflict in your home relationships, remember to practice love for each other. We show our love for each other by listening, praying, and caring. If our hearts not are open to doing these things, we are seriously broken as a family. We need God's love and forgiveness to heal us.

- **Be child friendly**—teach your children to *Listen Pray Care* for you. It is very important that they pray for those who are in authority over them. We all should learn this as little children because we need this skill for a lifetime of loving others.

- **Remember the goal**—everyone is listened to, prayed for, and cared for in our family. We accomplish this when everyone participates.

15
CHRISTIAN COACHES
TRAINING HEARTS

Athletic Coaches & Directors-Sports Camp
Directors-Sports Ministry Directors-Fitness
Trainers-Sports Coordinators-Referees

Some of my favorite coaches are wonderful models of
Christ. They describe themselves as Christians who
happen to coach. Their identity is in Christ. For them,
coaching is infinitely rewarding and a great privilege. As
a Christian coach, I'm sure you love what you do and are
always looking for ways to improve—just like your
athletes.

Listen Pray Care is a relational strategy that helps build relationships in our Christian ministries and sports activities. It is important to our development in body, mind, and spirit.

As you know, coaching goes beyond athletics to the development of character and wisdom. Christ commanded his disciples to show love for one another. It was the mark that set them apart. LPC focuses on the fundamentals, teaching good listening skills, a prayerful life, and the stewardship of our time, treasure, and talents to the good of our neighbor. LPC can help you effectively meet the goal of teammates showing Christian love for one another.

I receive frequent questions about working with non-believers. Here is a sample statement I developed for use by a Christian coach challenged with practicing LPC among those who do not believe in God:

> C: Although our athletic program is a Christian program, we understand that not all athletes on our teams have committed themselves to Christ and may have conflicting beliefs about God. While all people can benefit from the activities in LPC groups, praying to God is a matter of personal faith.
>
> We respect and understand that some athletes may need to pass when their turn comes to pray without discrimination or judgment.

We understand that each athlete's spiritual journey is in the hands of God. Our Christian athletes, of course, will be taught, encouraged, and expected to pray.

Easy Steps to Implement *Listen Pray Care*

- Study the background and content of LPC found in this book.

- Build LPC into your team goals and mission statements.

- Decide how you are going to implement LPC. If you already have small groups or huddles, this will be easier.

- Give instructions and oversee the process. Fundamentals are not taught overnight. All athletes benefit from coaching. When they forget, go back to the basics.

- Celebrate and affirm success.

Tips

- **Focus on the goal**—as everyone listens, prays, and cares; everyone is listened to, prayed for, and cared for.

- **Help develop identity**—as you work on developing and maturing your athletes in their identity, help them to identify their commitment to Christ as expressed in love for God and others. The answer to *how* they love one another should be simple, comprehensive, and concise—we *Listen Pray Care*.

- **Share the Gospel**—Jesus explains how we are to love each other. We are to love as he loved us. When we explain how he loved us through his death on the cross, we share the Gospel. Encourage your team to reflect the Good News of God's love in Christ in what they say and do.

- **Align LPC with your mission**—do the work of making sure your written statements about your mission, purpose and goals include learning and practicing LPC. It will make the transition to LPC in your team building strategy smoother. Since we live for Christ and thus give glory to God, the greatest command that governs all our behavior is love. We love one another as a team by practicing LPC.

- **Involve the parents**—explain in your parent meetings what you are doing and what they can expect. Offer suggestions for talking with their athletes about participating in LPC groups. Be especially clear about how you handle athletes of different faiths.

- **Go beyond small groups**—LPC in team huddles or small groups prepares teammates for loving others. Respecting and caring for athletes from other teams is part of our show of love for others.

- **Practice LPC on and off the field**—our willingness to love others is not to be limited to the sport, but it should be part of our daily lives as 24/7 Christian witnesses.

APPENDIX

Below, there are four Biblical illustrations of the key components to *Listen Pray Care* found in the ministry of Jesus and Paul.

FEEDING THE 5,000

Jesus and his disciples took a boat to a place away from the crowds. The crowds, however, ran ahead of him and were waiting when he arrived. Jesus had compassion on them and taught them. As the day drew to a close, this is what happened:

> By this time it was late in the day, so [Jesus']
> disciples came to him [**Listen**]. "This is a remote
> place," they said, "and it's already very late. Send
> the people away so that they can go to the
> surrounding countryside and villages and buy
> themselves something to eat."
> (Mark 6:35-36)

Jesus first challenged his disciples to feed the crowd. After their obvious objections, Jesus asked them how much food they had. They reported they had five loaves of bread and two fish. He responded in two ways. He expressed his relationship to God and his relationship to the people in need.

Taking the five loaves and the two fish he looked
up to heaven [*Pray*], he gave thanks and broke the
loaves. Then he gave them to his disciples to
distribute to the people [*Care*] (Mark 6:35-41).

LAZARUS

Jesus was some distance from the village of Bethany
where Lazarus lived. Word was sent to Jesus [*Listen*] by
two sisters, Mary and Martha:

Lord, the one you love is sick. (John 11:3)

But before Jesus made it back, Lazarus died. When
Jesus finally arrived, Martha said to him, "Lord, if
you had been here, my brother would not have
died. But I know that even now God will give you
whatever you ask." (John 11:21-22)

Martha's sister, Mary, also told Jesus:

Lord, if you had been here, my brother would not
have died. (John 11:32b)

Jesus asked to see the burial site. Upon arrival he
ordered them to remove the stone. Jesus lovingly
responded in two ways—vertically to God and
horizontally to the people as follows:

So they took away the stone. Then Jesus looked up [*Pray*] and said, "Father, I thank you that you have heard me. I knew that you always hear me, but I said this for the benefit of the people standing here, that they may believe that you sent me."

When he had said this, Jesus called in a loud voice, "Lazarus, come out!" The dead man came out [*Care*], his hands and feet wrapped with strips of linen, and a cloth around his face.

Jesus said to them, "Take off the grave clothes and let him go." (John 11:41-44)

THE DEAF MUTE

Another time, Jesus encountered a man that could not hear or speak:

There some people brought to [Jesus] a man who was deaf and could hardly talk, and they begged Jesus [*Listen*] to place his hand on him.

After he took him aside, away from the crowd, Jesus put his fingers into the man's ears. Then he spit and touched the man's tongue. He looked up to heaven [*Pray*] and with a deep sigh said to him, "Ephphatha!" (which means "Be opened!"). At this, the man's ears were opened, his tongue was loosened and he began to speak plainly [*Care*]. (Mark 7:32-35)

THE SICK FATHER

When Paul journeyed to the island of Malta, he responded with prayer and care in a similar fashion as Jesus. Here is the short account:

> There was an estate nearby that belonged to Publius, the chief official of the island. He welcomed us to his home and showed us generous hospitality for three days. His father was sick in bed, suffering from fever and dysentery. Paul went in to see him [*Listen*] and, after prayer [*Pray*], placed his hands on him and healed him [*Care*]. (Acts 28:7-8)

ABOUT THE AUTHOR

Rev. Alan Klatt is the founder of The LPC Project and
author of *Listen Pray Care,* adding to his multiple works
about Christian leadership, learning, and life. He has
served the Christian church for over 30 years as a pastor,
church planter, youth minister, worship leader,
musician, and high school religion teacher. He is a father
of eight children and calls the Milwaukee, Wisconsin
area home. Visit him at listenpraycare.org